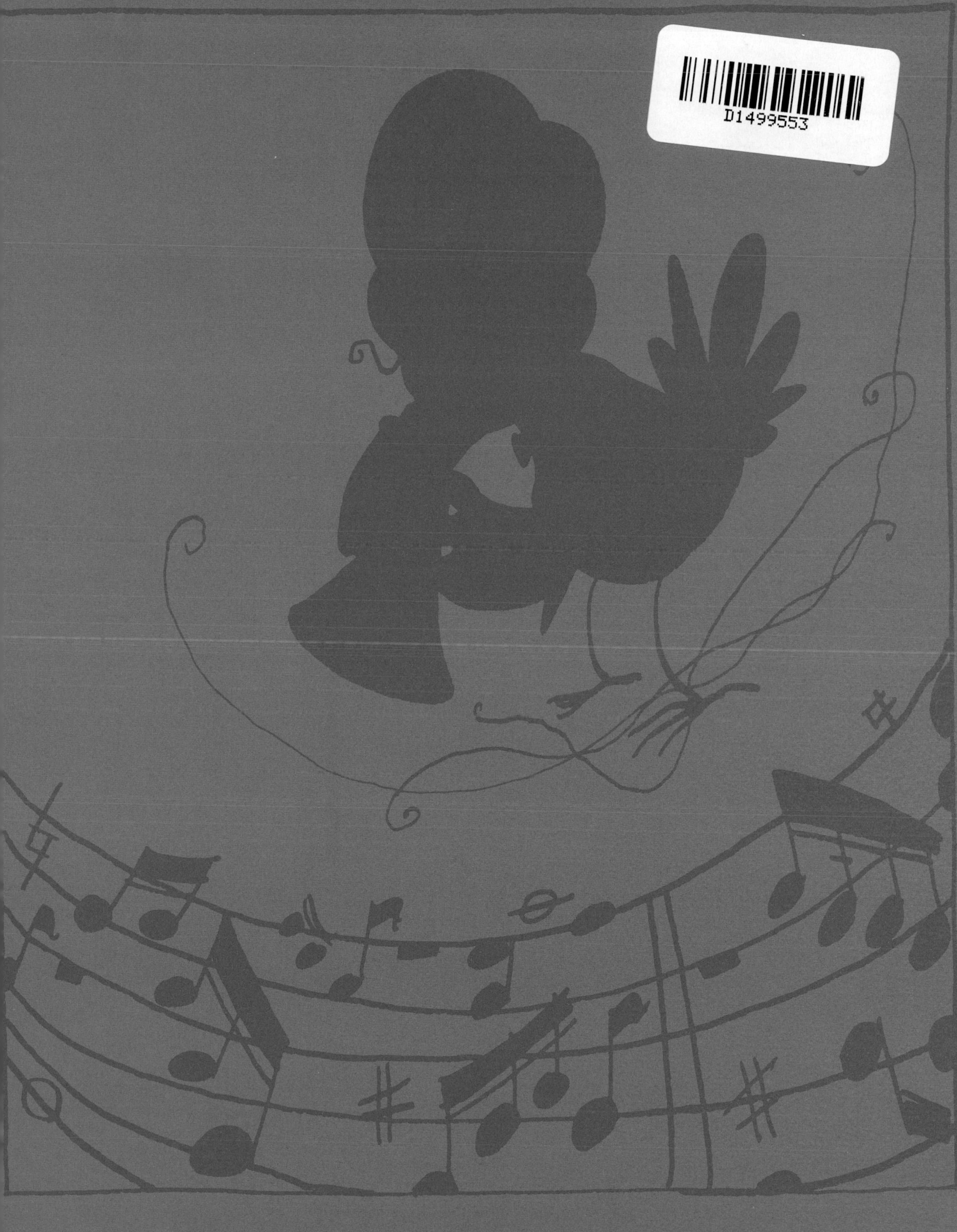

Betty Blues

ISBN 978-1-56163-758-4
Library of Congress Control Number: 2013944726
© 2003 Editions Paquet
www.paquet.li
Rights arranged through Sylvain Coissard Agency, France
© 2013 NBM for the English Translation
Translation by Joe Johnson
Lettering by Ortho

1st printing November 2013

Comicslit is an imprint
and trademark of

NANTIER · BEALL · MINOUSTCHINE
Publishing inc.
new york

Betty Blues

Renaud Dillies

Colors: Anne-Claire Jouvray

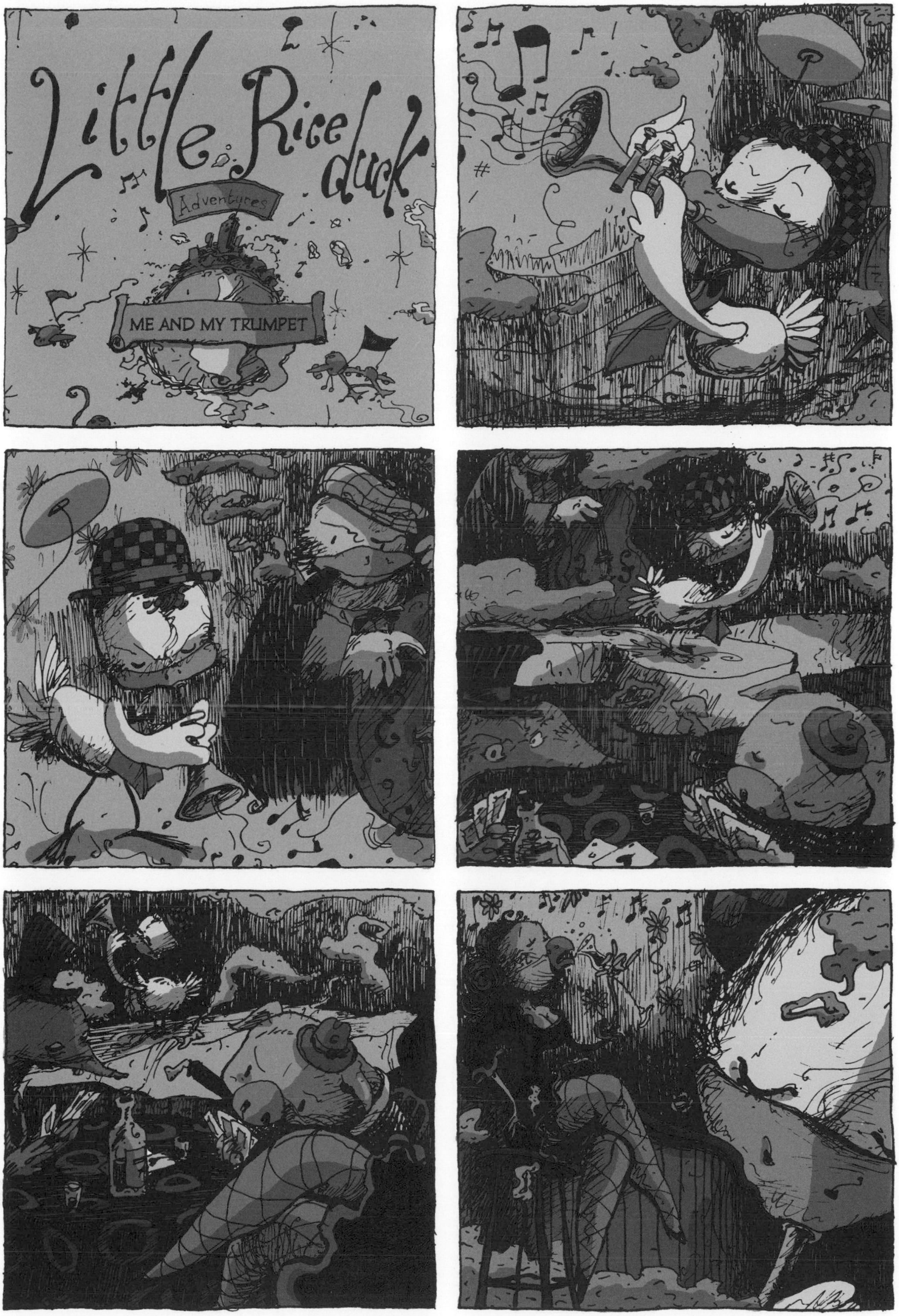
Little Rice duck
Adventures
ME AND MY TRUMPET

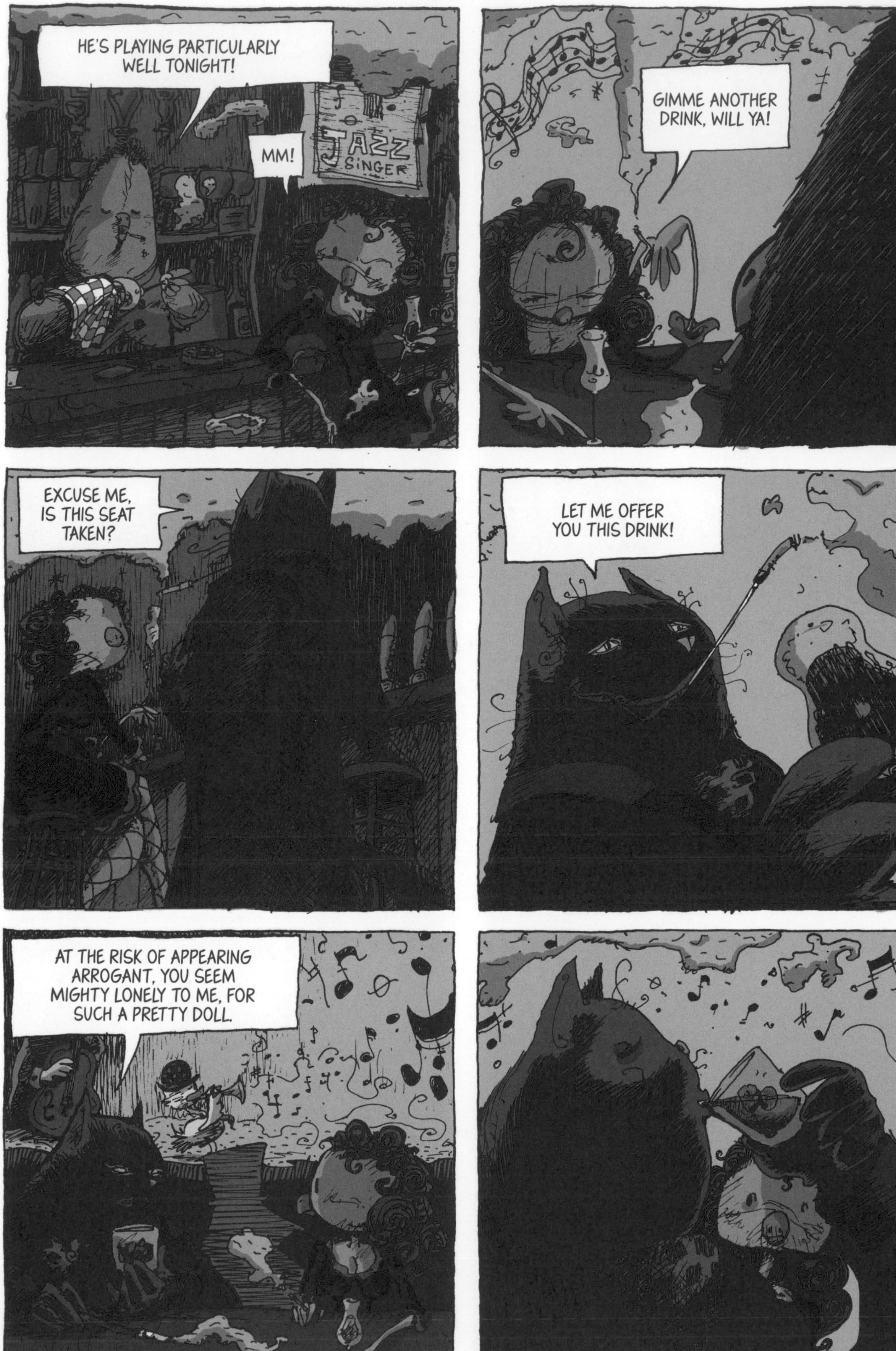
HE'S PLAYING PARTICULARLY WELL TONIGHT!
MM!
JAZZ SINGER
GIMME ANOTHER DRINK, WILL YA!
EXCUSE ME, IS THIS SEAT TAKEN?
LET ME OFFER YOU THIS DRINK!
AT THE RISK OF APPEARING ARROGANT, YOU SEEM MIGHTY LONELY TO ME, FOR SUCH A PRETTY DOLL.

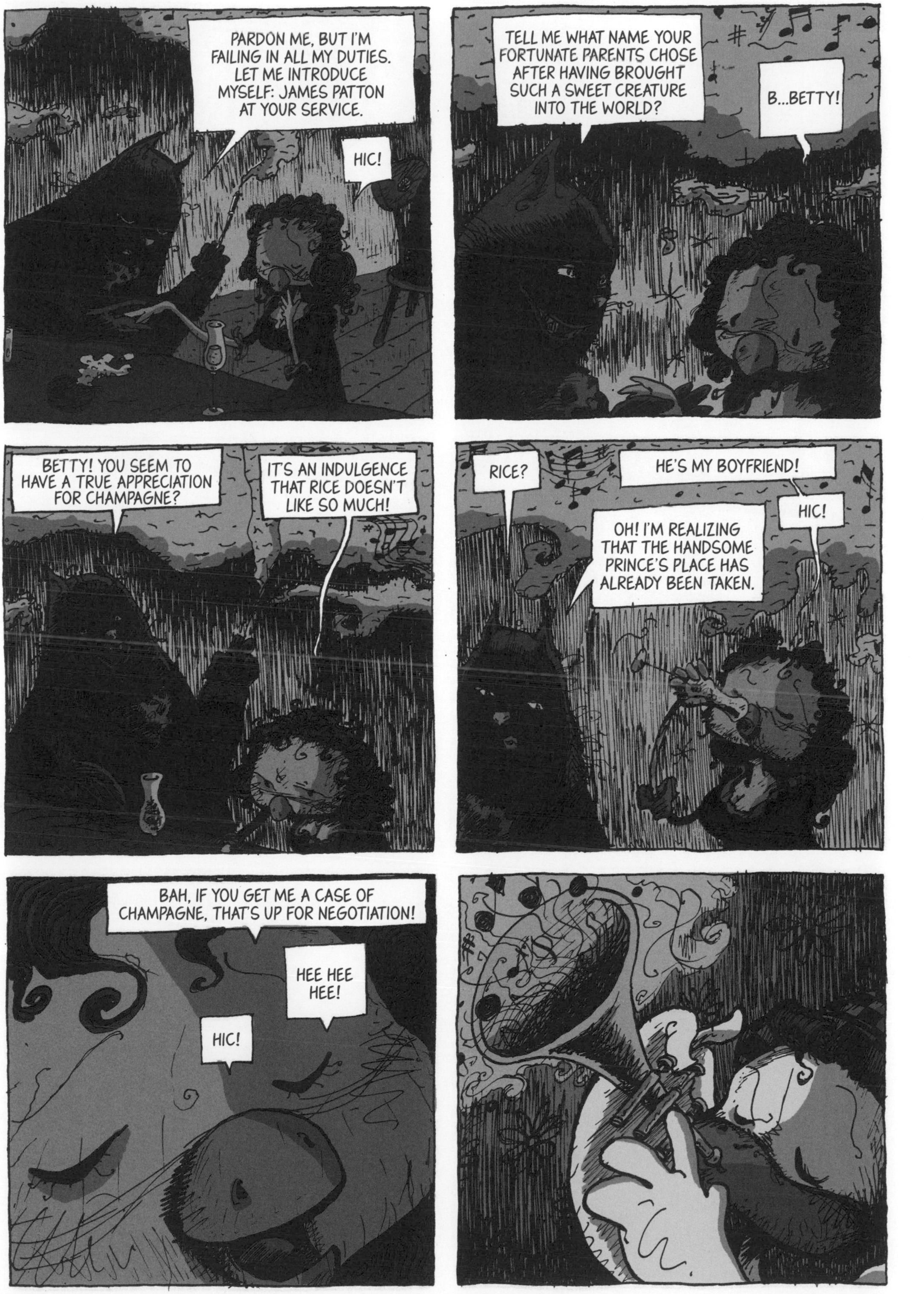

PARDON ME, BUT I'M FAILING IN ALL MY DUTIES. LET ME INTRODUCE MYSELF: JAMES PATTON AT YOUR SERVICE.
HIC!
TELL ME WHAT NAME YOUR FORTUNATE PARENTS CHOSE AFTER HAVING BROUGHT SUCH A SWEET CREATURE INTO THE WORLD?
B...BETTY!
BETTY! YOU SEEM TO HAVE A TRUE APPRECIATION FOR CHAMPAGNE?
IT'S AN INDULGENCE THAT RICE DOESN'T LIKE SO MUCH!
RICE?
HE'S MY BOYFRIEND!
HIC!
OH! I'M REALIZING THAT THE HANDSOME PRINCE'S PLACE HAS ALREADY BEEN TAKEN.
BAH, IF YOU GET ME A CASE OF CHAMPAGNE, THAT'S UP FOR NEGOTIATION!
HEE HEE HEE!
HIC!

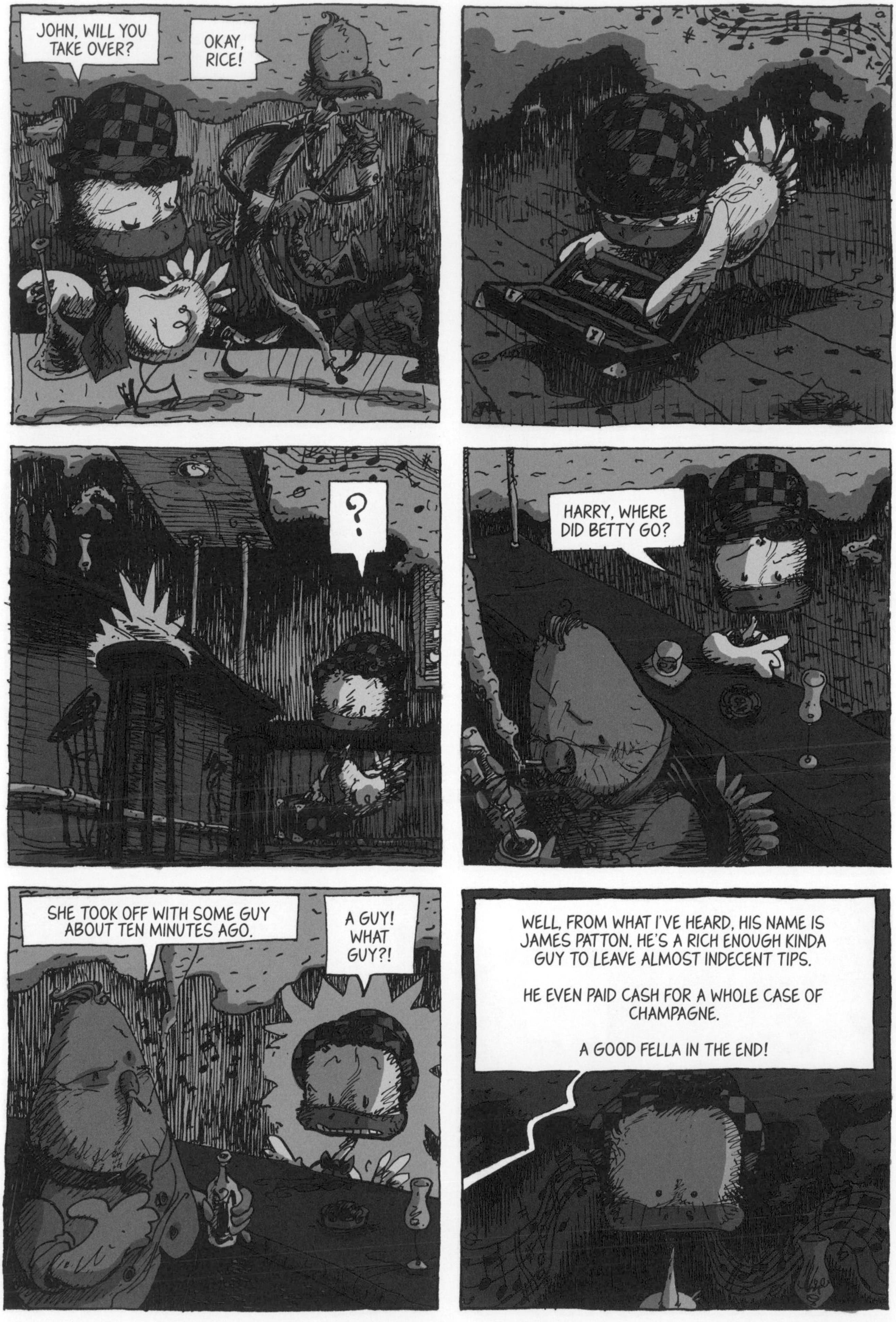
JOHN, WILL YOU TAKE OVER?
OKAY, RICE!
?
HARRY, WHERE DID BETTY GO?
SHE TOOK OFF WITH SOME GUY ABOUT TEN MINUTES AGO.
A GUY! WHAT GUY?!
WELL, FROM WHAT I'VE HEARD, HIS NAME IS JAMES PATTON. HE'S A RICH ENOUGH KINDA GUY TO LEAVE ALMOST INDECENT TIPS.
HE EVEN PAID CASH FOR A WHOLE CASE OF CHAMPAGNE.
A GOOD FELLA IN THE END!

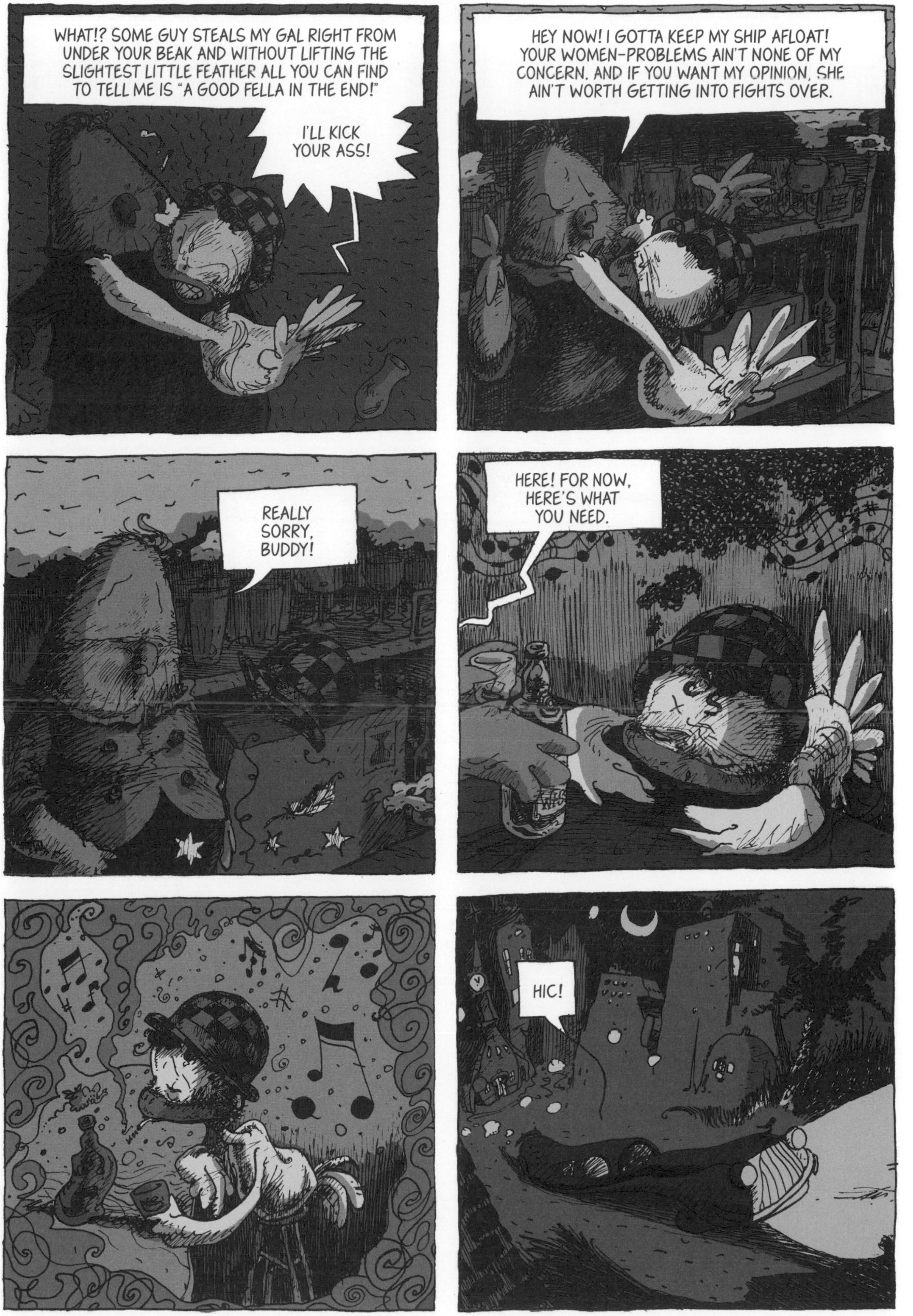
WHAT!? SOME GUY STEALS MY GAL RIGHT FROM UNDER YOUR BEAK AND WITHOUT LIFTING THE SLIGHTEST LITTLE FEATHER ALL YOU CAN FIND TO TELL ME IS "A GOOD FELLA IN THE END!"
I'LL KICK YOUR ASS!
HEY NOW! I GOTTA KEEP MY SHIP AFLOAT! YOUR WOMEN-PROBLEMS AIN'T NONE OF MY CONCERN. AND IF YOU WANT MY OPINION, SHE AIN'T WORTH GETTING INTO FIGHTS OVER.
REALLY SORRY, BUDDY!
HERE! FOR NOW, HERE'S WHAT YOU NEED.
HIC!

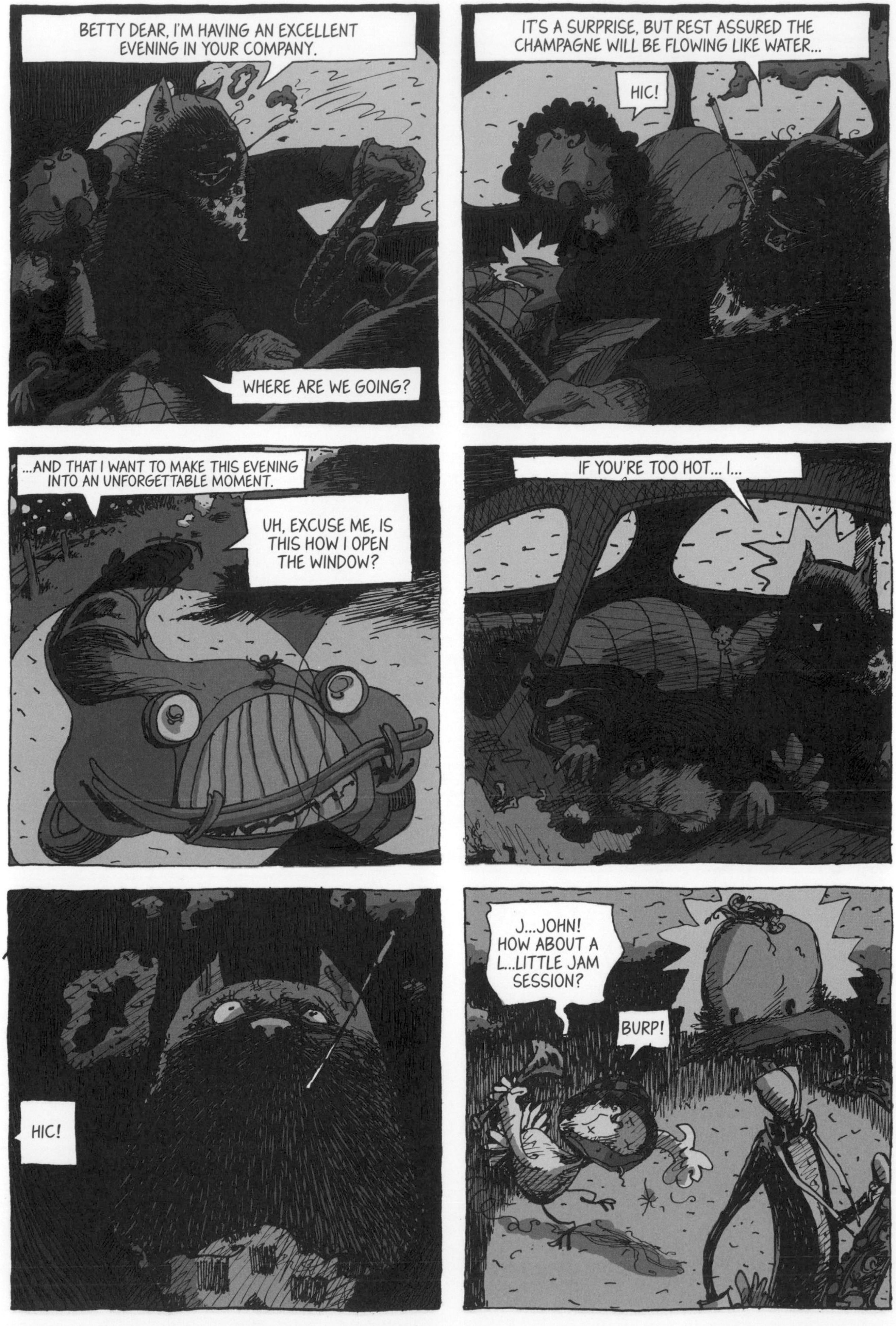

BETTY DEAR, I'M HAVING AN EXCELLENT EVENING IN YOUR COMPANY.
WHERE ARE WE GOING?
IT'S A SURPRISE, BUT REST ASSURED THE CHAMPAGNE WILL BE FLOWING LIKE WATER...
HIC!
...AND THAT I WANT TO MAKE THIS EVENING INTO AN UNFORGETTABLE MOMENT.
UH, EXCUSE ME, IS THIS HOW I OPEN THE WINDOW?
IF YOU'RE TOO HOT... I...
HIC!
J...JOHN! HOW ABOUT A L...LITTLE JAM SESSION?
BURP!

OWW!
B... BETTY!
CHARLIE! COME GIMME A HAND...WILL YA?!
B.
WELL NOW, YOU'RE PRETTY SMASHED, RICE!
BETTY...

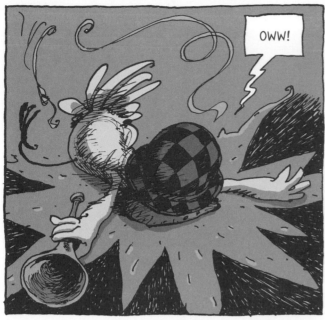

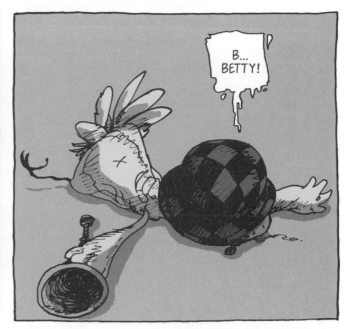

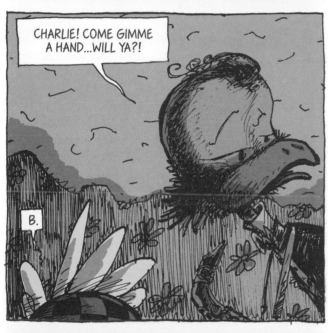

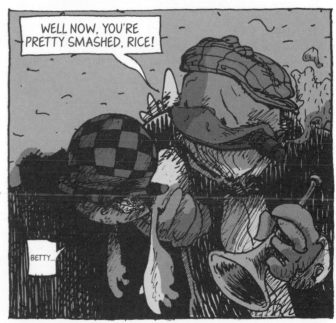

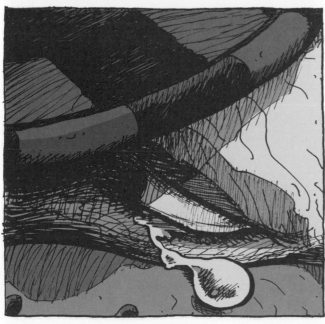

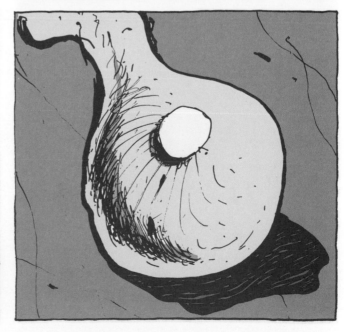

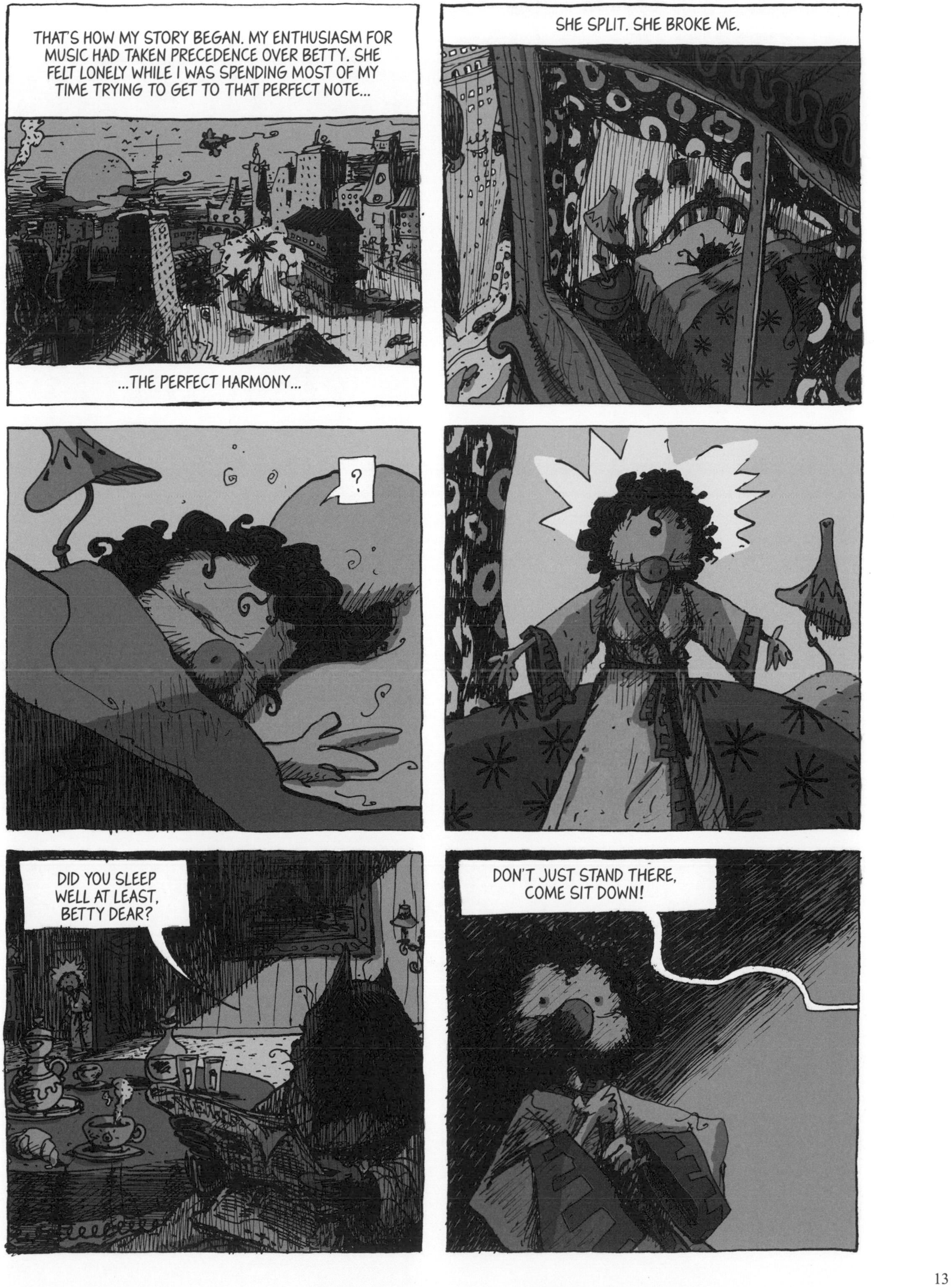
THAT'S HOW MY STORY BEGAN. MY ENTHUSIASM FOR MUSIC HAD TAKEN PRECEDENCE OVER BETTY. SHE FELT LONELY WHILE I WAS SPENDING MOST OF MY TIME TRYING TO GET TO THAT PERFECT NOTE...
...THE PERFECT HARMONY...
SHE SPLIT. SHE BROKE ME.
?
DID YOU SLEEP WELL AT LEAST, BETTY DEAR?
DON'T JUST STAND THERE, COME SIT DOWN!

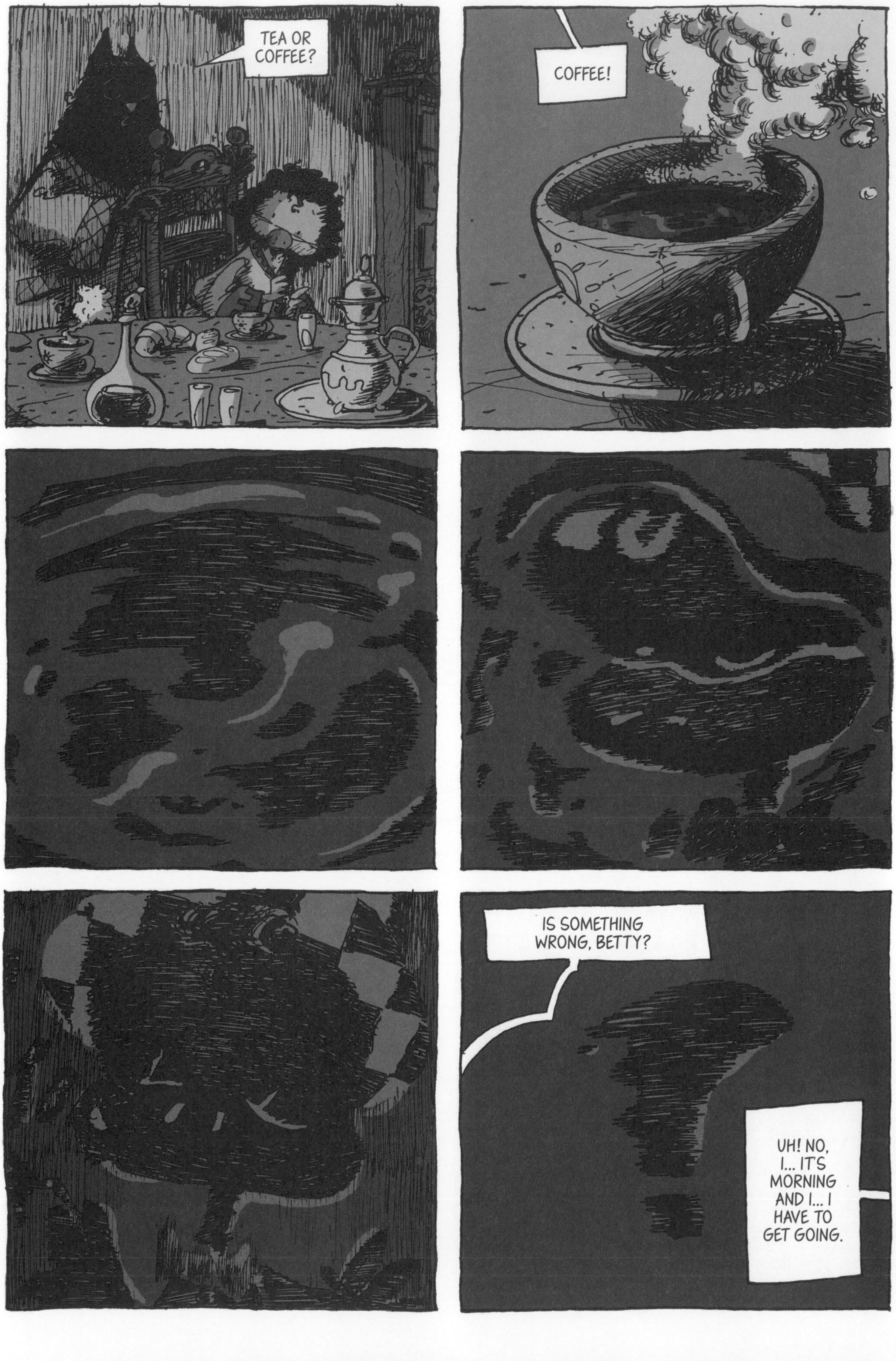
TEA OR COFFEE?
COFFEE!
IS SOMETHING WRONG, BETTY?
UH! NO, I... IT'S MORNING AND I... I HAVE TO GET GOING.

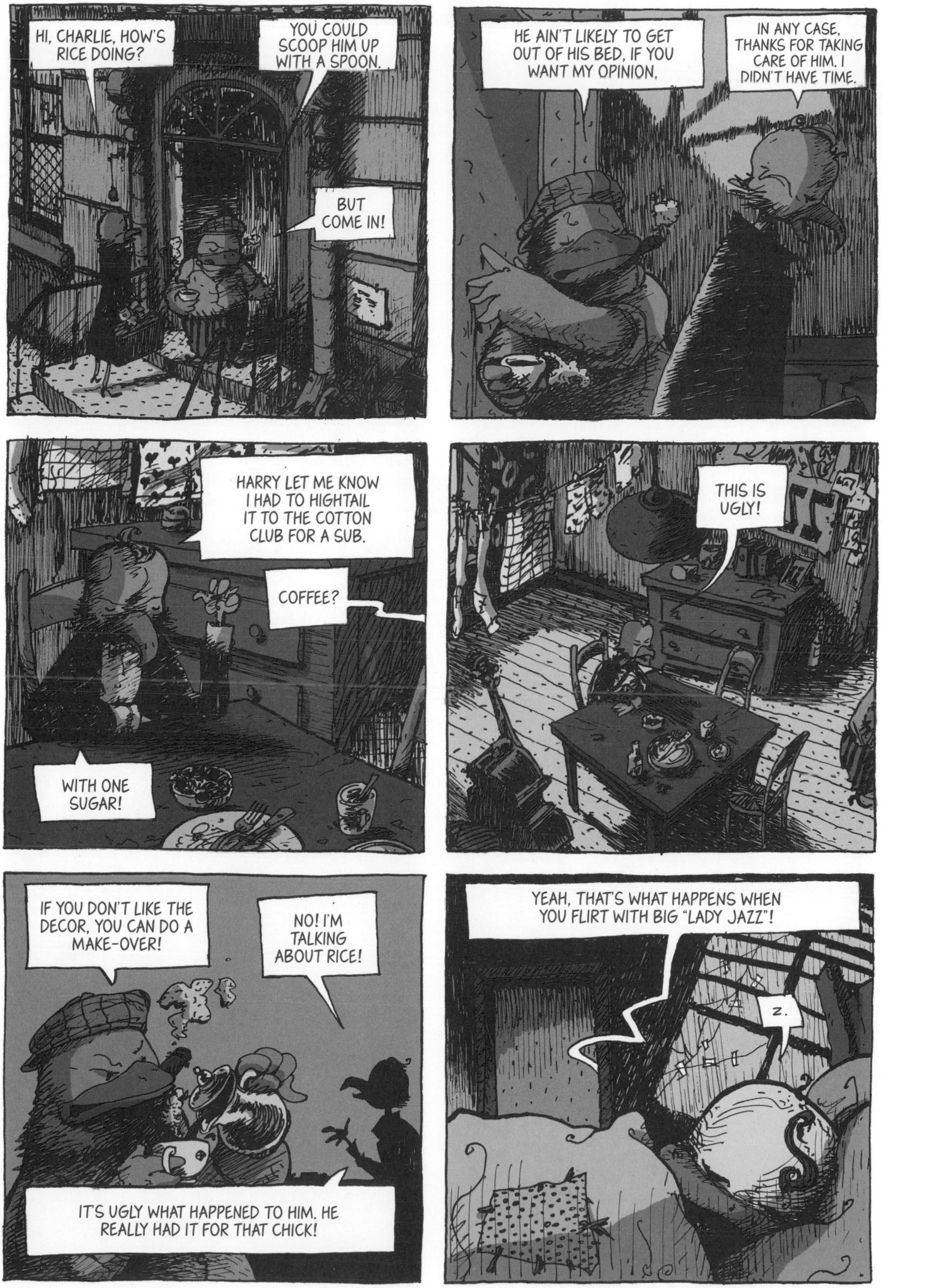
HI, CHARLIE, HOW'S RICE DOING?
YOU COULD SCOOP HIM UP WITH A SPOON.
BUT COME IN!
HE AIN'T LIKELY TO GET OUT OF HIS BED, IF YOU WANT MY OPINION.
IN ANY CASE, THANKS FOR TAKING CARE OF HIM. I DIDN'T HAVE TIME.
HARRY LET ME KNOW I HAD TO HIGHTAIL IT TO THE COTTON CLUB FOR A SUB.
COFFEE?
WITH ONE SUGAR!
THIS IS UGLY!
IF YOU DON'T LIKE THE DECOR, YOU CAN DO A MAKE-OVER!
NO! I'M TALKING ABOUT RICE!
IT'S UGLY WHAT HAPPENED TO HIM. HE REALLY HAD IT FOR THAT CHICK!
YEAH, THAT'S WHAT HAPPENS WHEN YOU FLIRT WITH BIG "LADY JAZZ"!
Z.

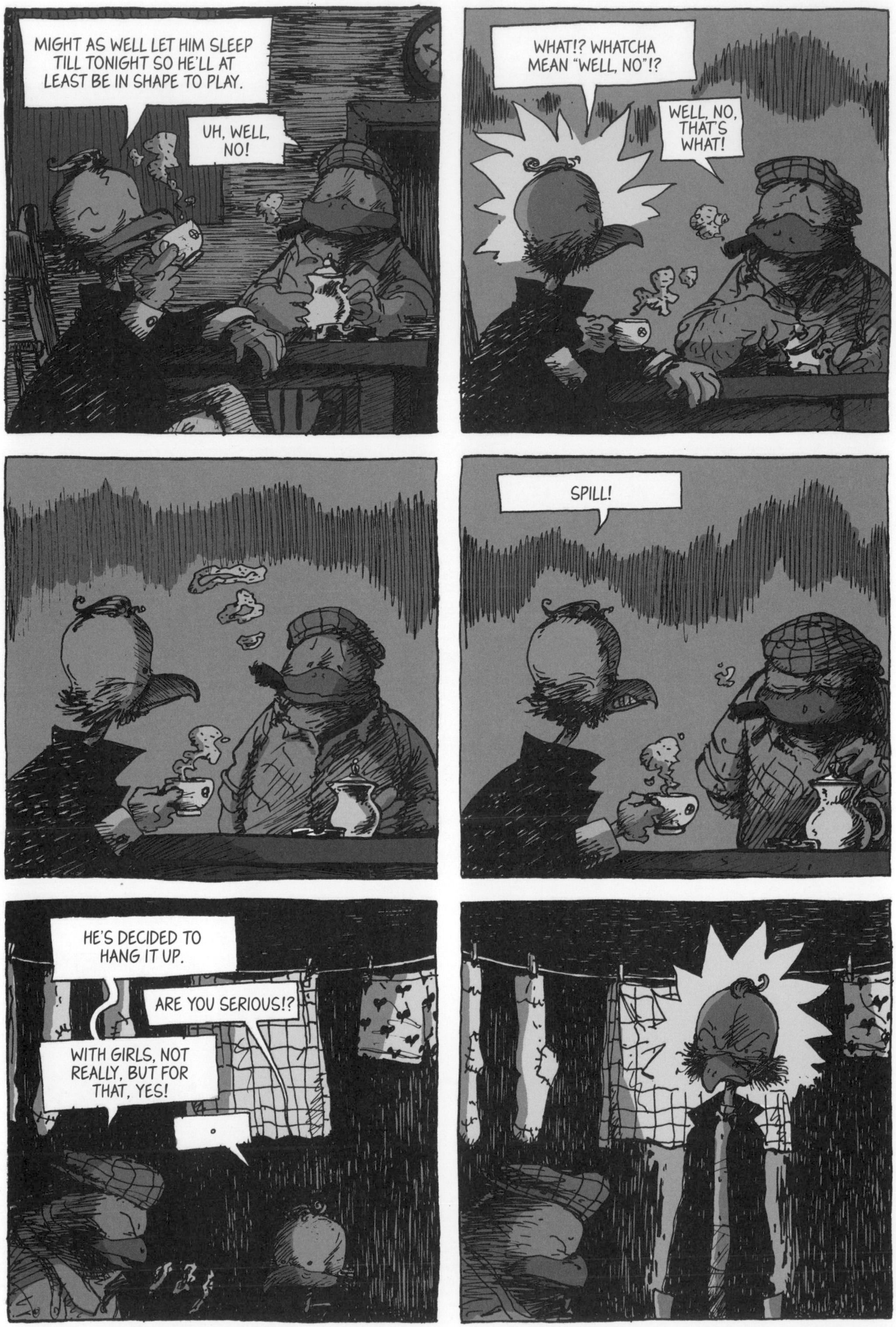
MIGHT AS WELL LET HIM SLEEP TILL TONIGHT SO HE'LL AT LEAST BE IN SHAPE TO PLAY.
UH, WELL, NO!
WHAT!? WHATCHA MEAN "WELL, NO"!?
WELL, NO, THAT'S WHAT!
SPILL!
HE'S DECIDED TO HANG IT UP.
ARE YOU SERIOUS!?
WITH GIRLS, NOT REALLY, BUT FOR THAT, YES!
o

GET UP!

WHAT'S THIS I'M HEARING?!

?

MISTER RICE IS DOING HIS PROUD DUCK, DECIDING TO STOP EVERYTHING JUST LIKE THAT!?!

MISTER RICE DOESN'T BOTHER ASKING WHETHER THAT PUTS OTHER FOLKS IN A BIND OR NOT!?

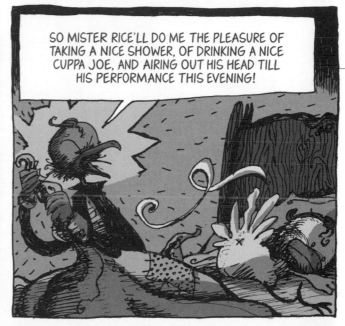

SO MISTER RICE'LL DO ME THE PLEASURE OF TAKING A NICE SHOWER, OF DRINKING A NICE CUPPA JOE, AND AIRING OUT HIS HEAD TILL HIS PERFORMANCE THIS EVENING!

WELL...LET'S JUST SAY IT'S GONNA BE A LITTLE COMPLICATED, YOU SEE, JOHN...

BECAUSE LAST NIGHT, I DID SOMETHING UNCOOL!

CHARLIE AND I WERE ON A BRIDGE, AND...

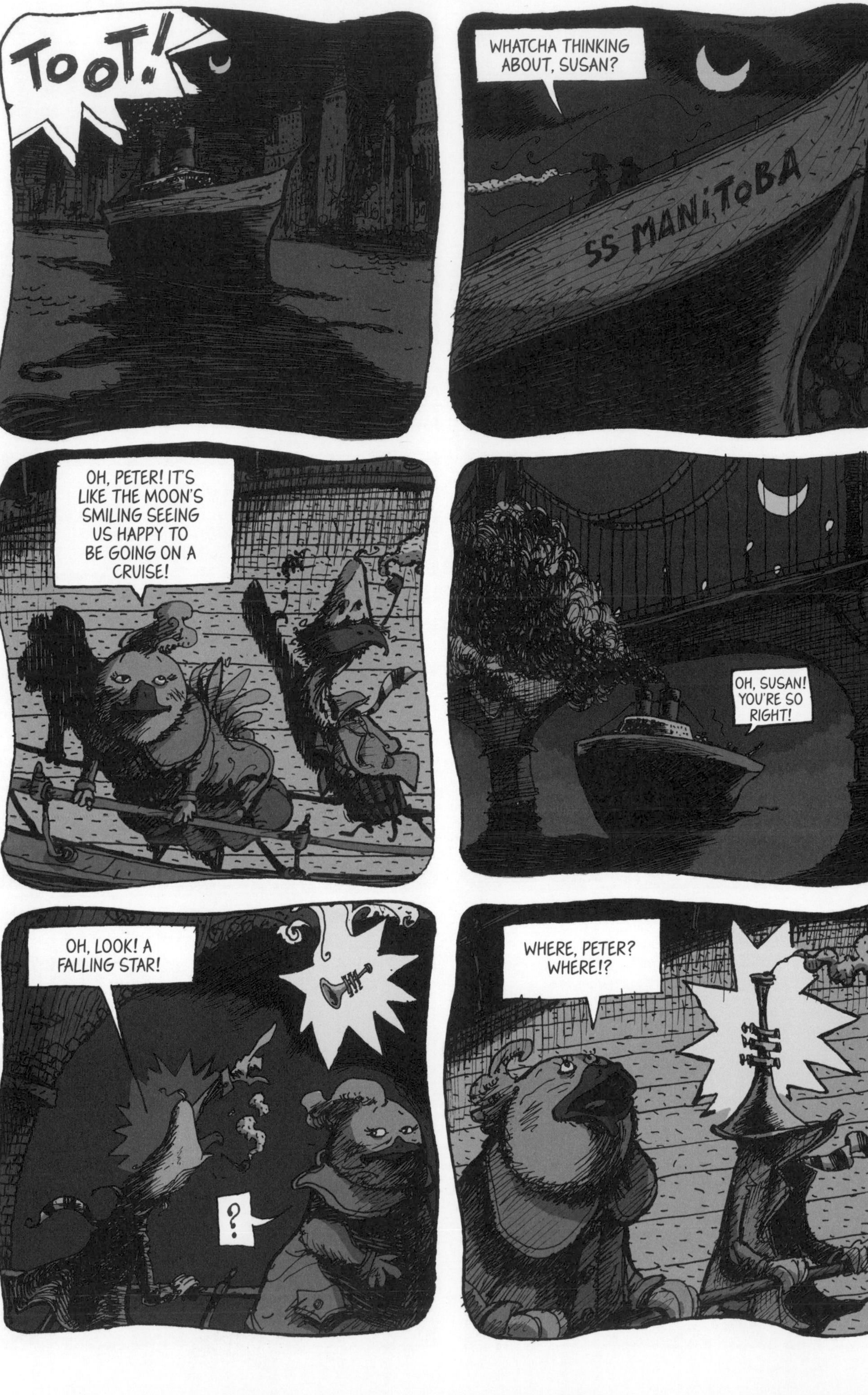
TOOT!
WHATCHA THINKING ABOUT, SUSAN?
SS MANITOBA
OH, PETER! IT'S LIKE THE MOON'S SMILING SEEING US HAPPY TO BE GOING ON A CRUISE!
OH, SUSAN! YOU'RE SO RIGHT!
OH, LOOK! A FALLING STAR!
?
WHERE, PETER? WHERE!?

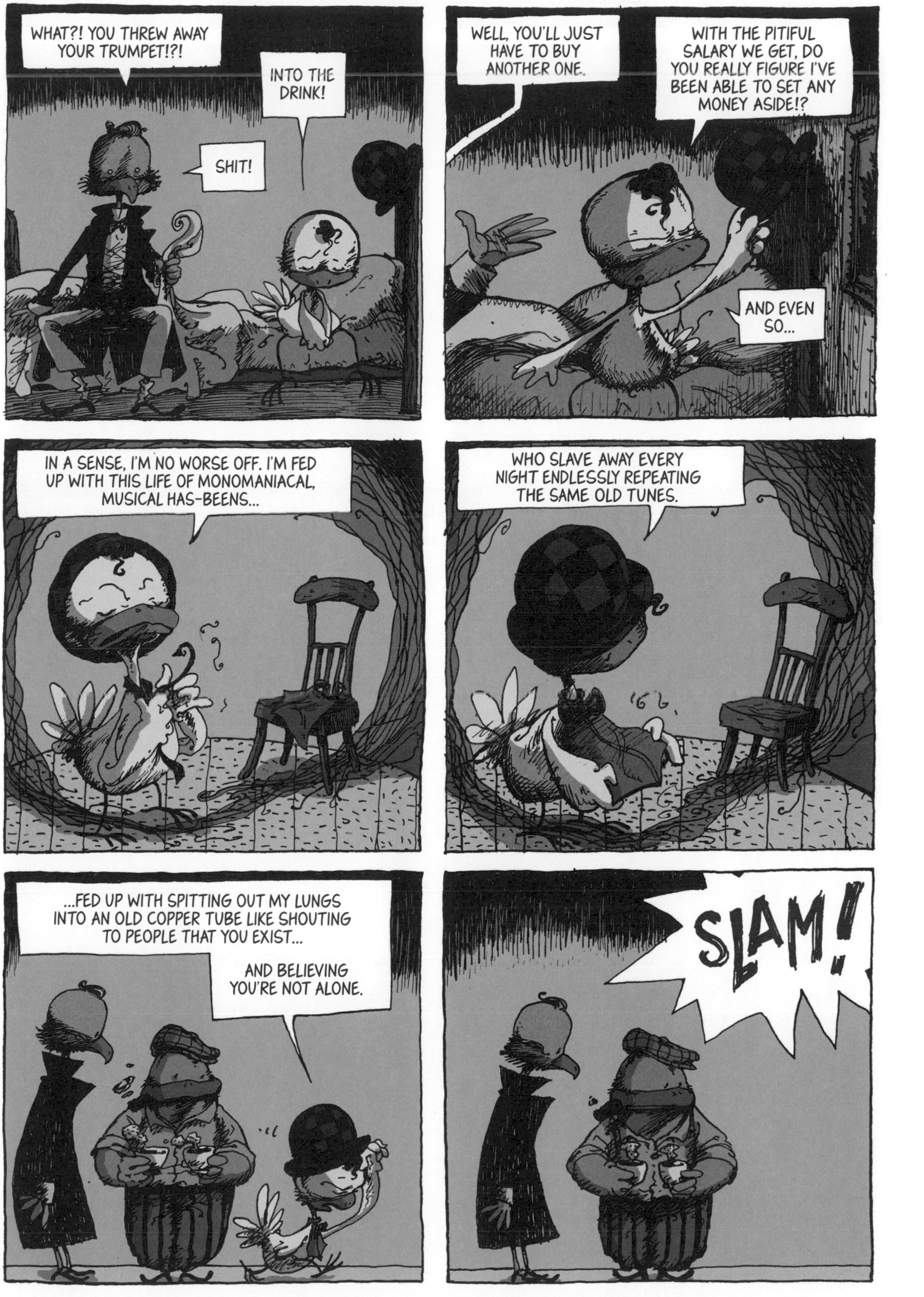

WHAT?! YOU THREW AWAY YOUR TRUMPET!?!
INTO THE DRINK!
SHIT!
WELL, YOU'LL JUST HAVE TO BUY ANOTHER ONE.
WITH THE PITIFUL SALARY WE GET, DO YOU REALLY FIGURE I'VE BEEN ABLE TO SET ANY MONEY ASIDE!?
AND EVEN SO...
IN A SENSE, I'M NO WORSE OFF. I'M FED UP WITH THIS LIFE OF MONOMANIACAL, MUSICAL HAS-BEENS...
WHO SLAVE AWAY EVERY NIGHT ENDLESSLY REPEATING THE SAME OLD TUNES.
...FED UP WITH SPITTING OUT MY LUNGS INTO AN OLD COPPER TUBE LIKE SHOUTING TO PEOPLE THAT YOU EXIST...
AND BELIEVING YOU'RE NOT ALONE.
SLAM!

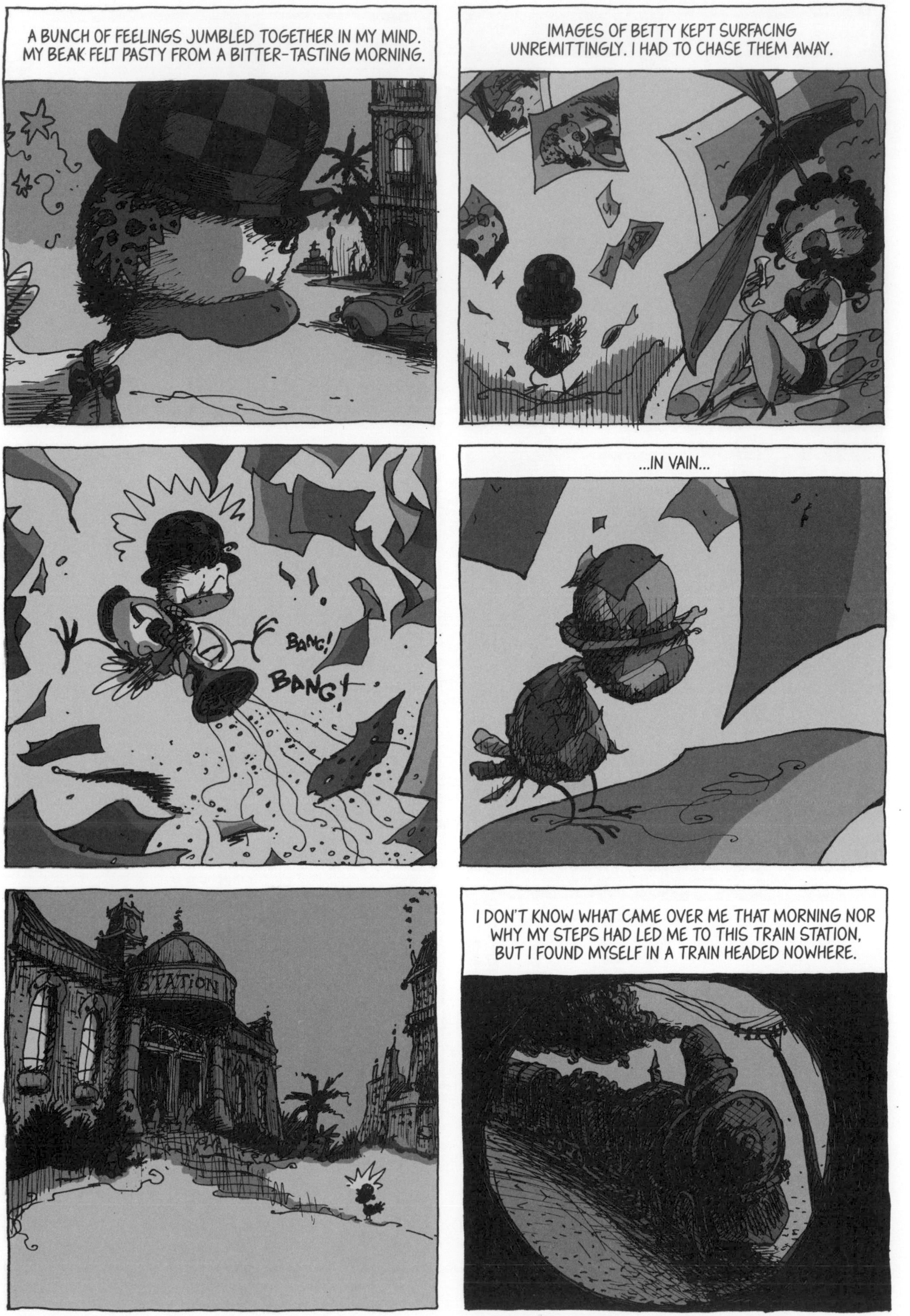
A BUNCH OF FEELINGS JUMBLED TOGETHER IN MY MIND. MY BEAK FELT PASTY FROM A BITTER-TASTING MORNING.
IMAGES OF BETTY KEPT SURFACING UNREMITTINGLY. I HAD TO CHASE THEM AWAY.
BANG!
BANG!
...IN VAIN...
STATION
I DON'T KNOW WHAT CAME OVER ME THAT MORNING NOR WHY MY STEPS HAD LED ME TO THIS TRAIN STATION, BUT I FOUND MYSELF IN A TRAIN HEADED NOWHERE.

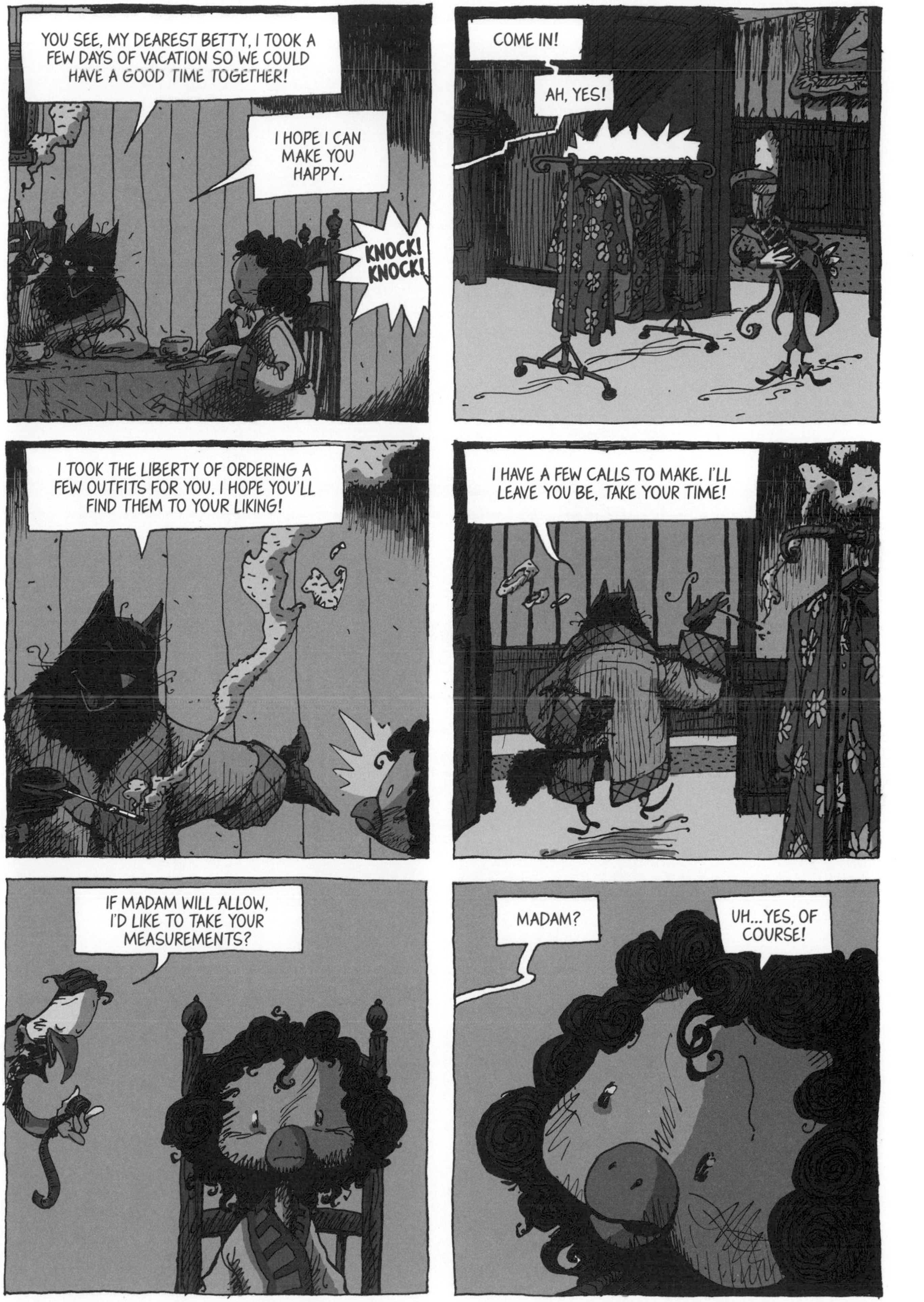

YOU SEE, MY DEAREST BETTY, I TOOK A FEW DAYS OF VACATION SO WE COULD HAVE A GOOD TIME TOGETHER!
I HOPE I CAN MAKE YOU HAPPY.
KNOCK! KNOCK!
COME IN!
AH, YES!
I TOOK THE LIBERTY OF ORDERING A FEW OUTFITS FOR YOU. I HOPE YOU'LL FIND THEM TO YOUR LIKING!
I HAVE A FEW CALLS TO MAKE. I'LL LEAVE YOU BE, TAKE YOUR TIME!
IF MADAM WILL ALLOW, I'D LIKE TO TAKE YOUR MEASUREMENTS?
MADAM?
UH... YES, OF COURSE!

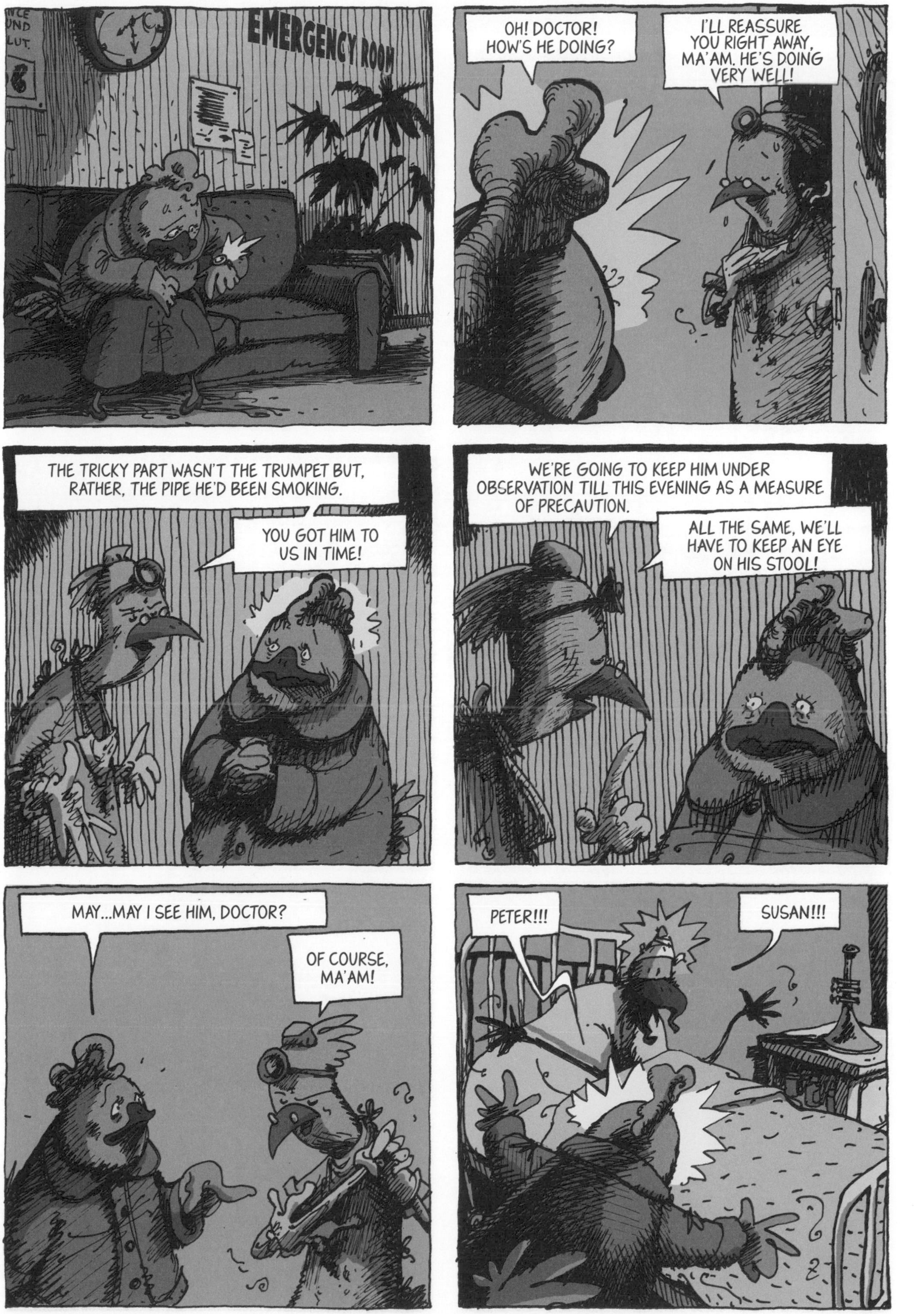
EMERGENCY ROOM
OH! DOCTOR! HOW'S HE DOING?
I'LL REASSURE YOU RIGHT AWAY, MA'AM. HE'S DOING VERY WELL!
THE TRICKY PART WASN'T THE TRUMPET BUT, RATHER, THE PIPE HE'D BEEN SMOKING.
YOU GOT HIM TO US IN TIME!
WE'RE GOING TO KEEP HIM UNDER OBSERVATION TILL THIS EVENING AS A MEASURE OF PRECAUTION.
ALL THE SAME, WE'LL HAVE TO KEEP AN EYE ON HIS STOOL!
MAY...MAY I SEE HIM, DOCTOR?
OF COURSE, MA'AM!
PETER!!!
SUSAN!!!

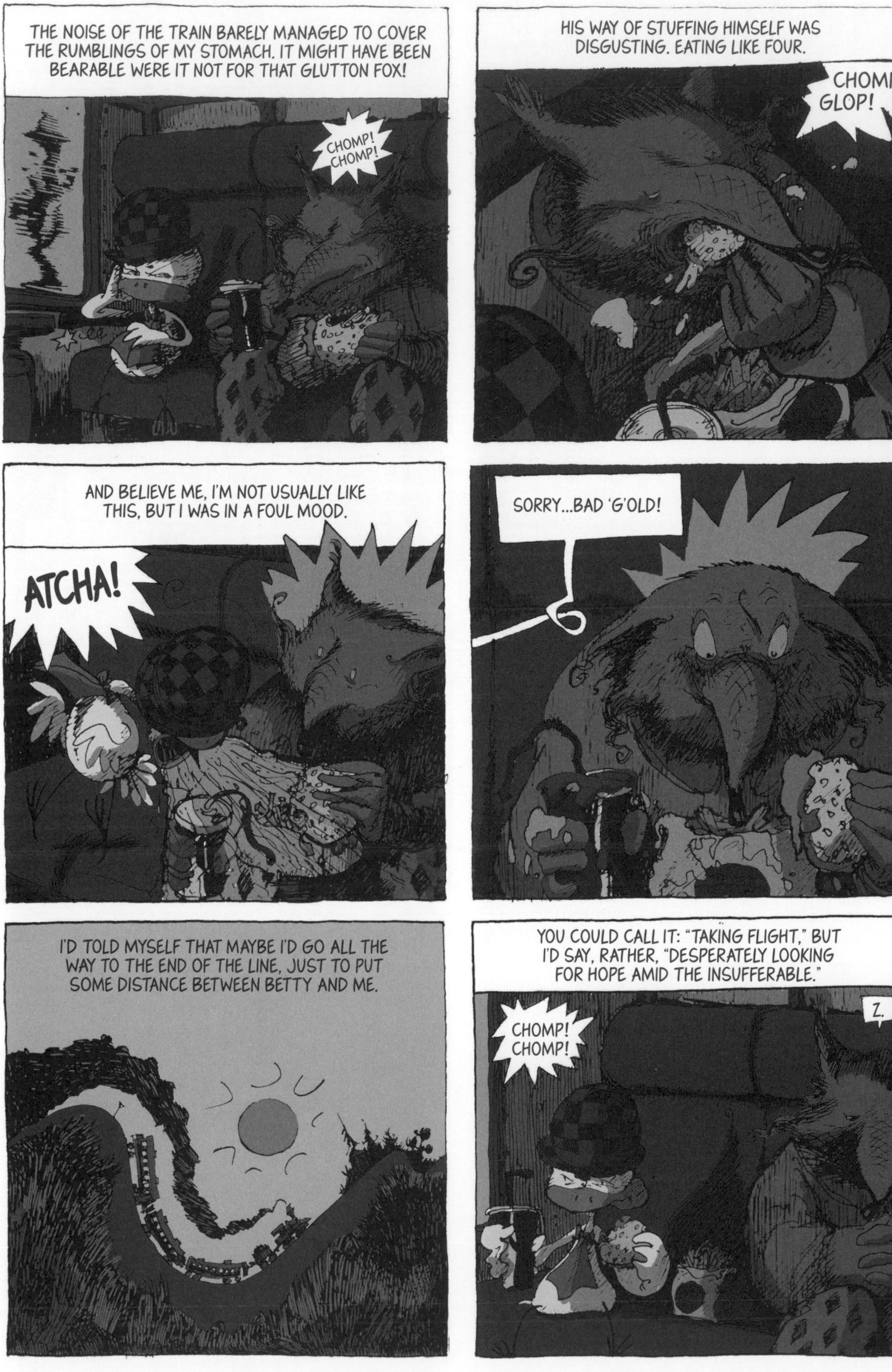
THE NOISE OF THE TRAIN BARELY MANAGED TO COVER THE RUMBLINGS OF MY STOMACH. IT MIGHT HAVE BEEN BEARABLE WERE IT NOT FOR THAT GLUTTON FOX!
CHOMP! CHOMP!
HIS WAY OF STUFFING HIMSELF WAS DISGUSTING. EATING LIKE FOUR.
CHOMP! GLOP!
AND BELIEVE ME, I'M NOT USUALLY LIKE THIS, BUT I WAS IN A FOUL MOOD.
ATCHA!
SORRY...BAD 'G'OLD!
I'D TOLD MYSELF THAT MAYBE I'D GO ALL THE WAY TO THE END OF THE LINE, JUST TO PUT SOME DISTANCE BETWEEN BETTY AND ME.
YOU COULD CALL IT: "TAKING FLIGHT," BUT I'D SAY, RATHER, "DESPERATELY LOOKING FOR HOPE AMID THE INSUFFERABLE."
CHOMP! CHOMP!
Z.

I WATCHED THE LANDSCAPE ZIPPING BY WITH THAT FEELING YOU SOMETIMES GET THAT IT'S AS THOUGH SOMEONE WERE UNROLLING A STAGE SET AROUND A MOTIONLESS TRAIN.

THE THROBBING RHYTHM OF THE TRAIN GOT THE BETTER OF ME...I ENDED UP NODDING OFF.

TÔTAKTATÔᴼᴼᴼOM!

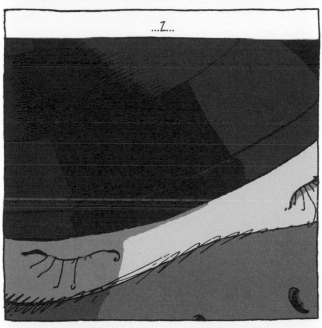

...Z...

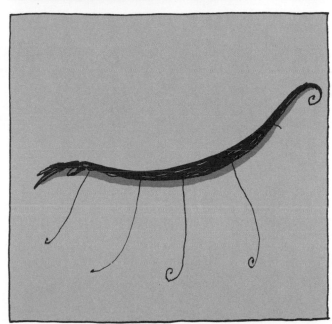

I WATCHED THE LANDSCAPE ZIPPING BY WITH THAT FEELING YOU SOMETIMES GET THAT IT'S AS THOUGH SOMEONE WERE UNROLLING A STAGE SET AROUND A MOTIONLESS TRAIN.

THE THROBBING RHYTHM OF THE TRAIN GOT THE BETTER OF ME...I ENDED UP NODDING OFF.

25

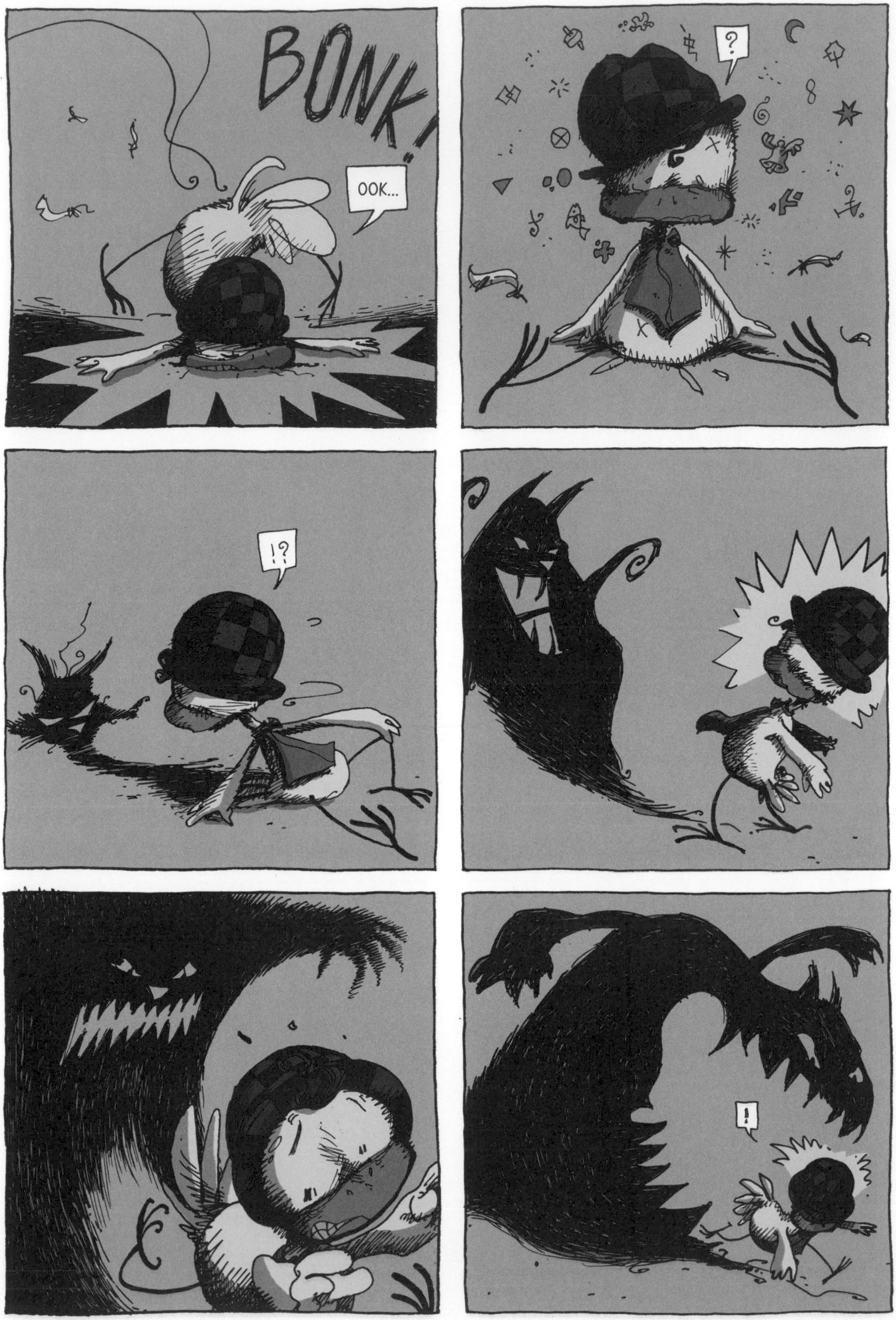
BONK!
OOK...
?
!?
!

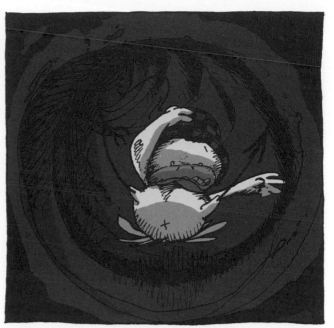

SPLOT!

WELL, LOOK AT THAT!

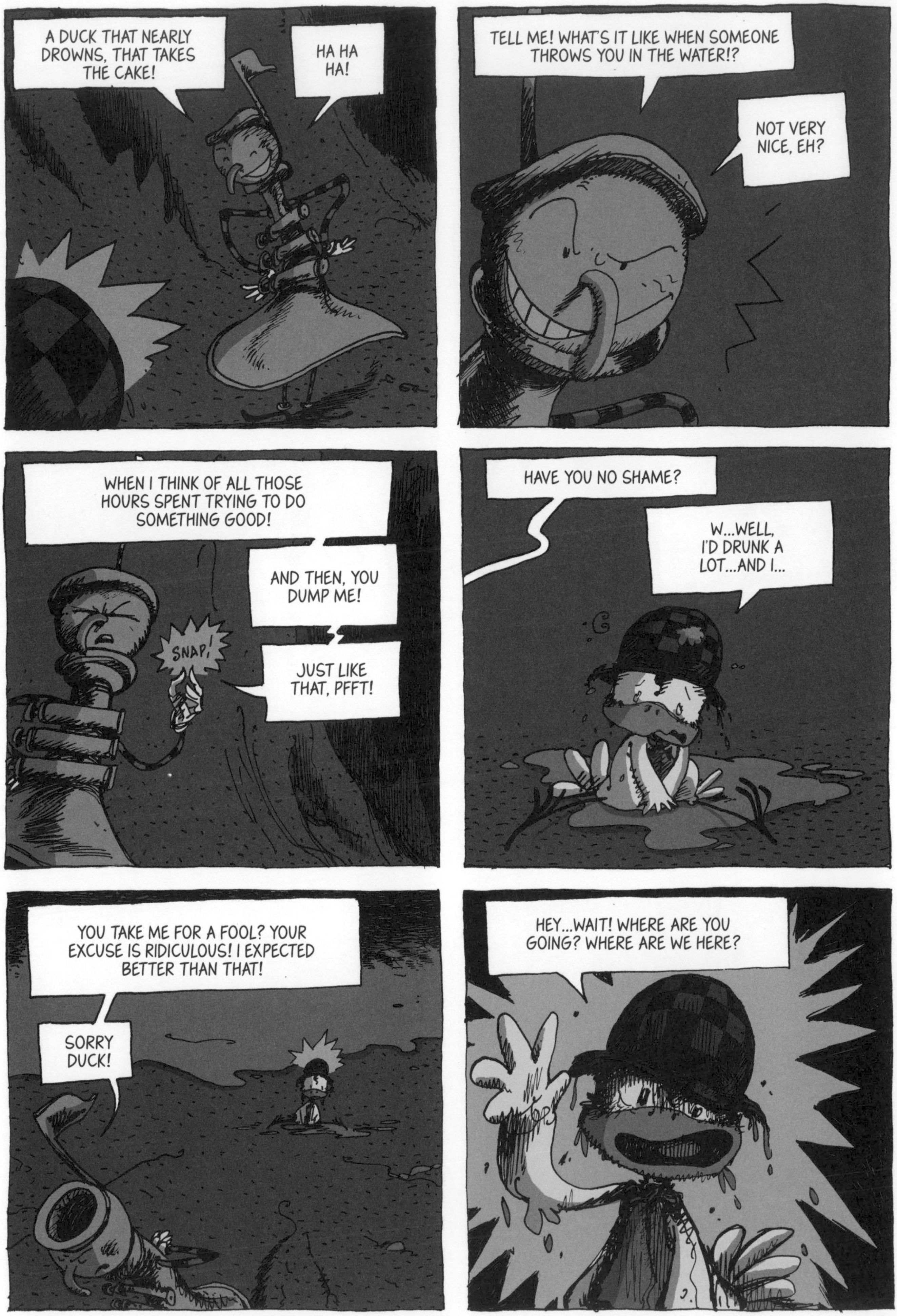
A DUCK THAT NEARLY DROWNS, THAT TAKES THE CAKE!
HA HA HA!
TELL ME! WHAT'S IT LIKE WHEN SOMEONE THROWS YOU IN THE WATER!?
NOT VERY NICE, EH?
WHEN I THINK OF ALL THOSE HOURS SPENT TRYING TO DO SOMETHING GOOD!
AND THEN, YOU DUMP ME!
SNAP!
JUST LIKE THAT, PFFT!
HAVE YOU NO SHAME?
W...WELL, I'D DRUNK A LOT...AND I...
YOU TAKE ME FOR A FOOL? YOUR EXCUSE IS RIDICULOUS! I EXPECTED BETTER THAN THAT!
SORRY DUCK!
HEY...WAIT! WHERE ARE YOU GOING? WHERE ARE WE HERE?

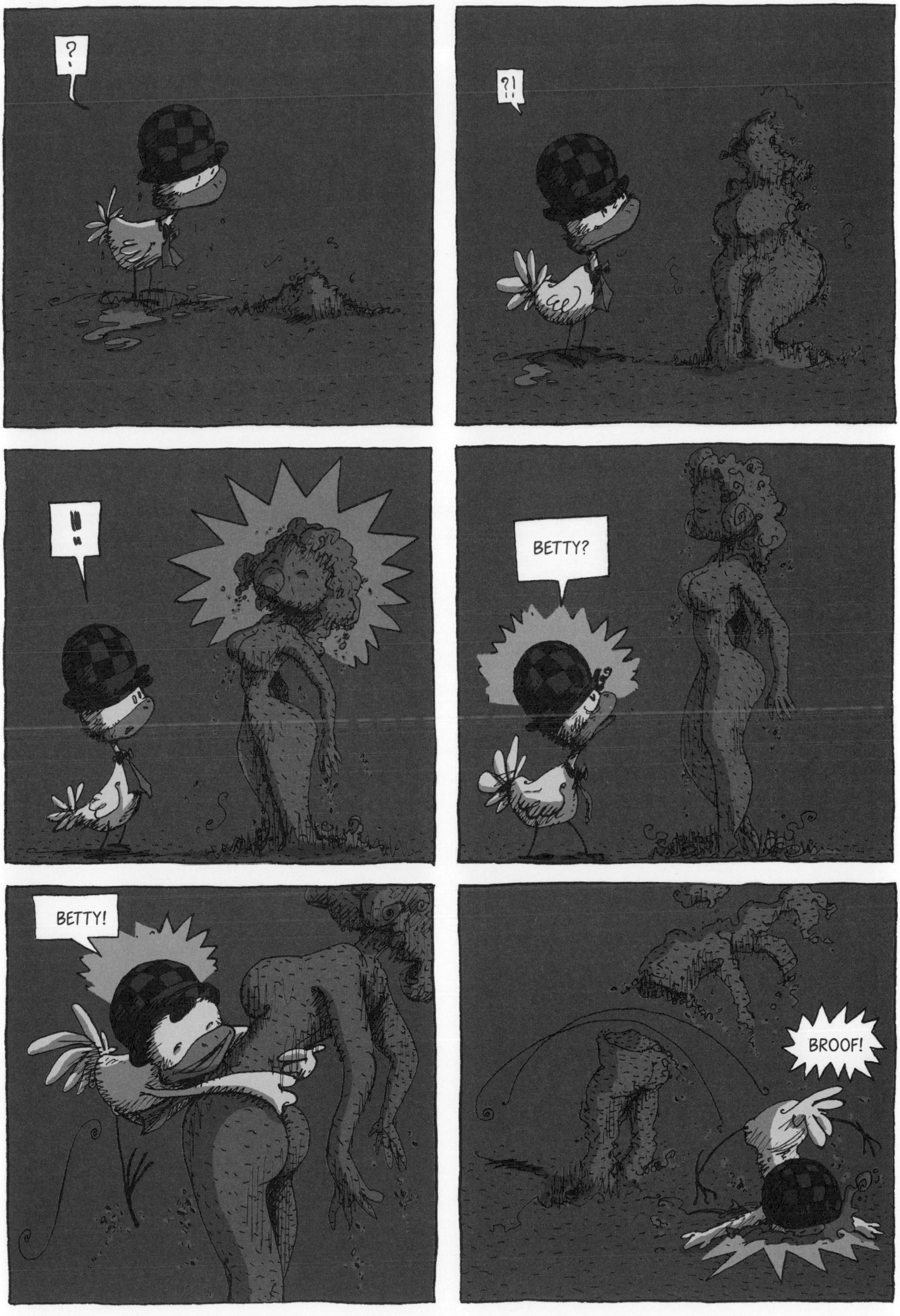
?
?!
!!
BETTY?
BETTY!
BROOF!

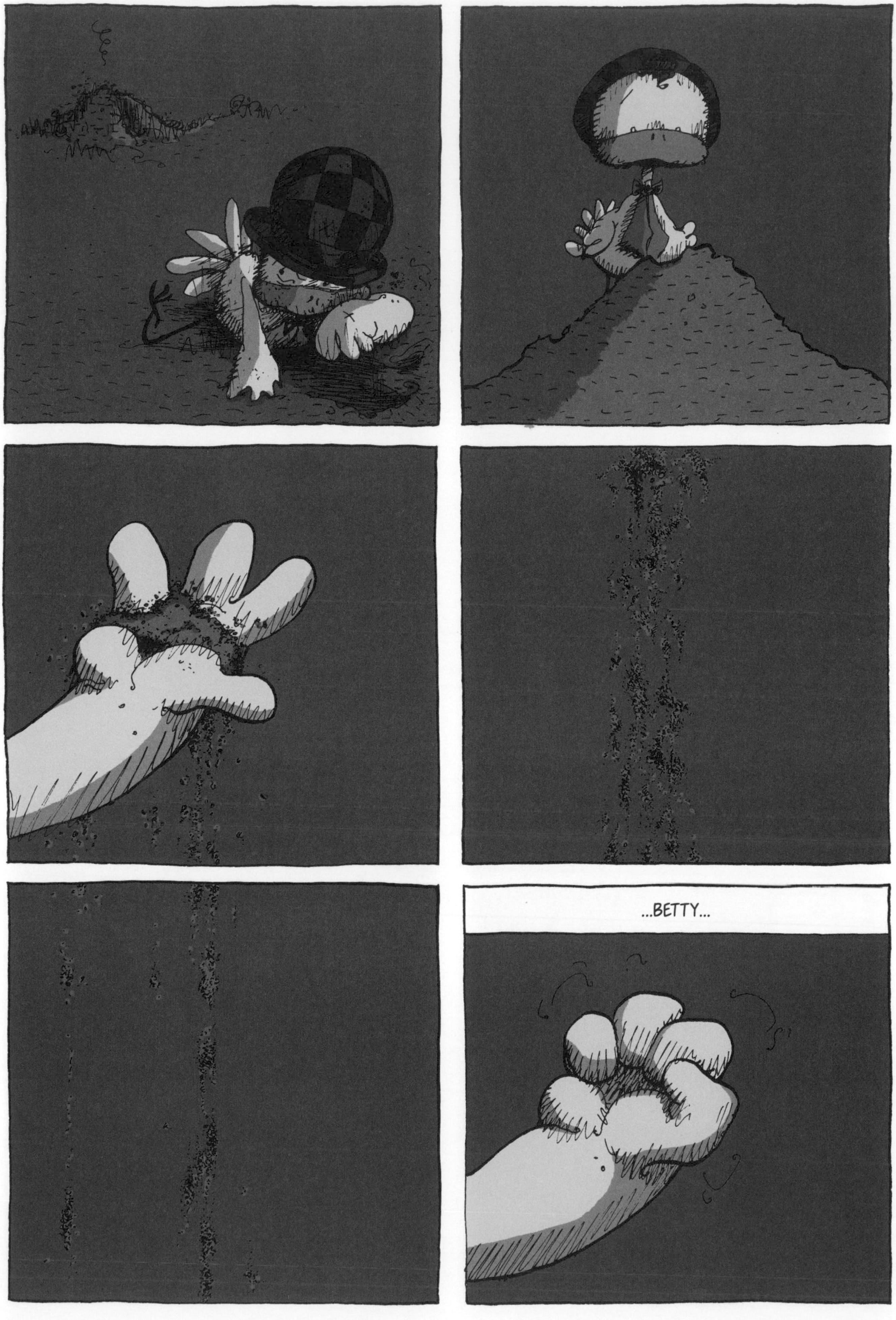
...BETTY...

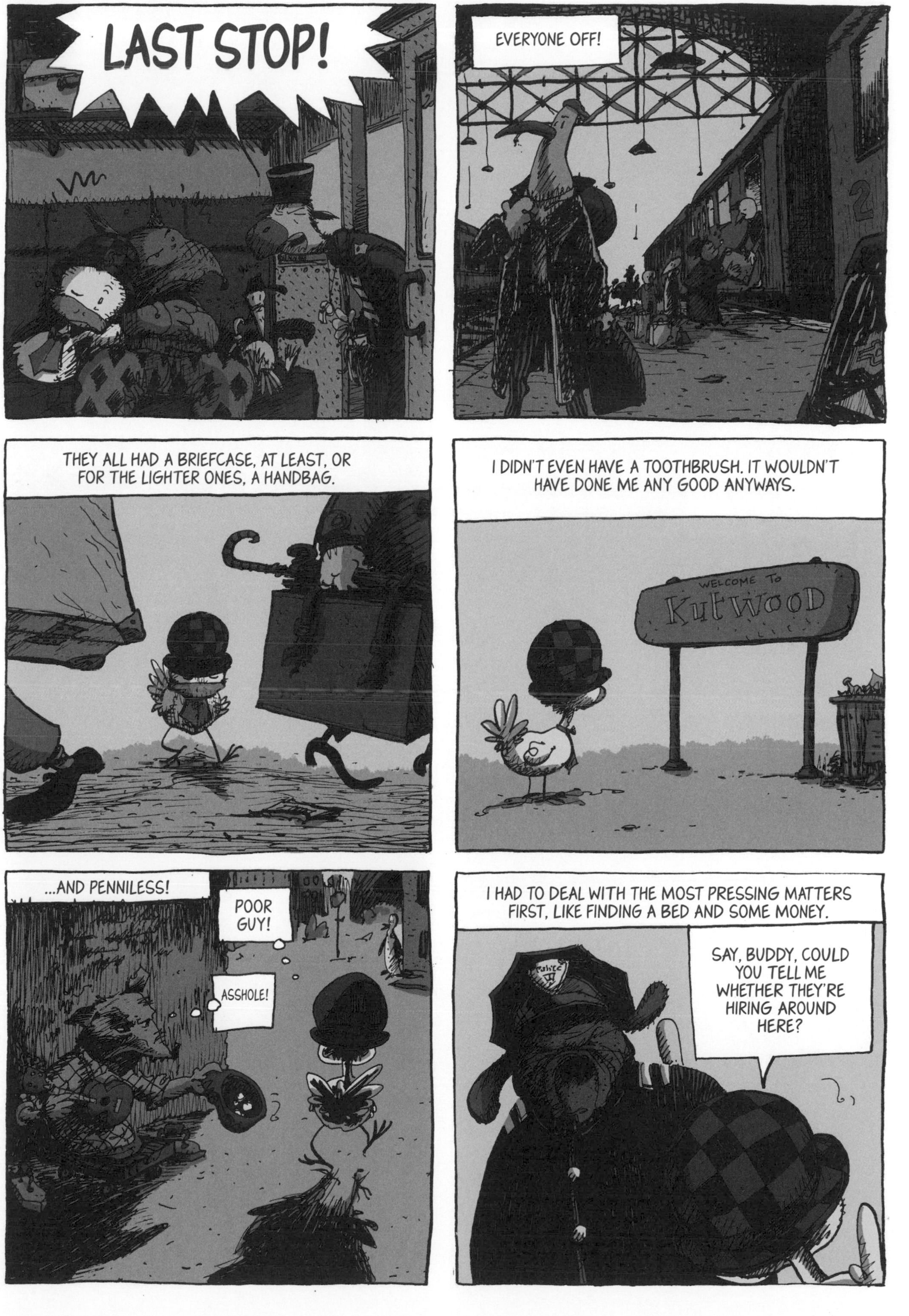
LAST STOP!
EVERYONE OFF!
THEY ALL HAD A BRIEFCASE, AT LEAST, OR FOR THE LIGHTER ONES, A HANDBAG.
I DIDN'T EVEN HAVE A TOOTHBRUSH. IT WOULDN'T HAVE DONE ME ANY GOOD ANYWAYS.
WELCOME TO
KUTWOOD
...AND PENNILESS!
POOR GUY!
ASSHOLE!
I HAD TO DEAL WITH THE MOST PRESSING MATTERS FIRST, LIKE FINDING A BED AND SOME MONEY.
SAY, BUDDY, COULD YOU TELL ME WHETHER THEY'RE HIRING AROUND HERE?

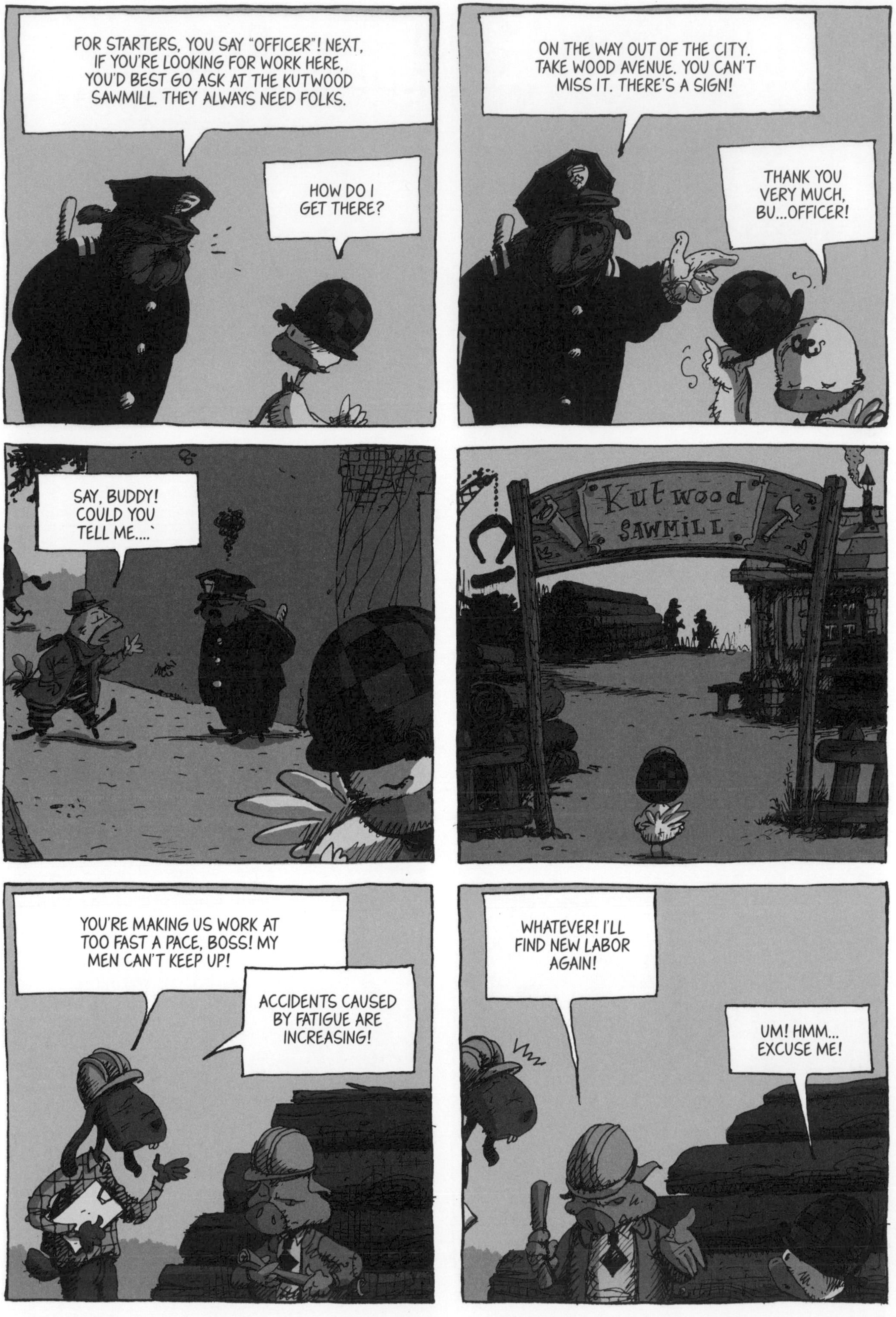
FOR STARTERS, YOU SAY "OFFICER"! NEXT, IF YOU'RE LOOKING FOR WORK HERE, YOU'D BEST GO ASK AT THE KUTWOOD SAWMILL. THEY ALWAYS NEED FOLKS.
HOW DO I GET THERE?
ON THE WAY OUT OF THE CITY. TAKE WOOD AVENUE. YOU CAN'T MISS IT. THERE'S A SIGN!
THANK YOU VERY MUCH, BU...OFFICER!
SAY, BUDDY! COULD YOU TELL ME....
Kutwood SAWMILL
YOU'RE MAKING US WORK AT TOO FAST A PACE, BOSS! MY MEN CAN'T KEEP UP!
ACCIDENTS CAUSED BY FATIGUE ARE INCREASING!
WHATEVER! I'LL FIND NEW LABOR AGAIN!
UM! HMM... EXCUSE ME!

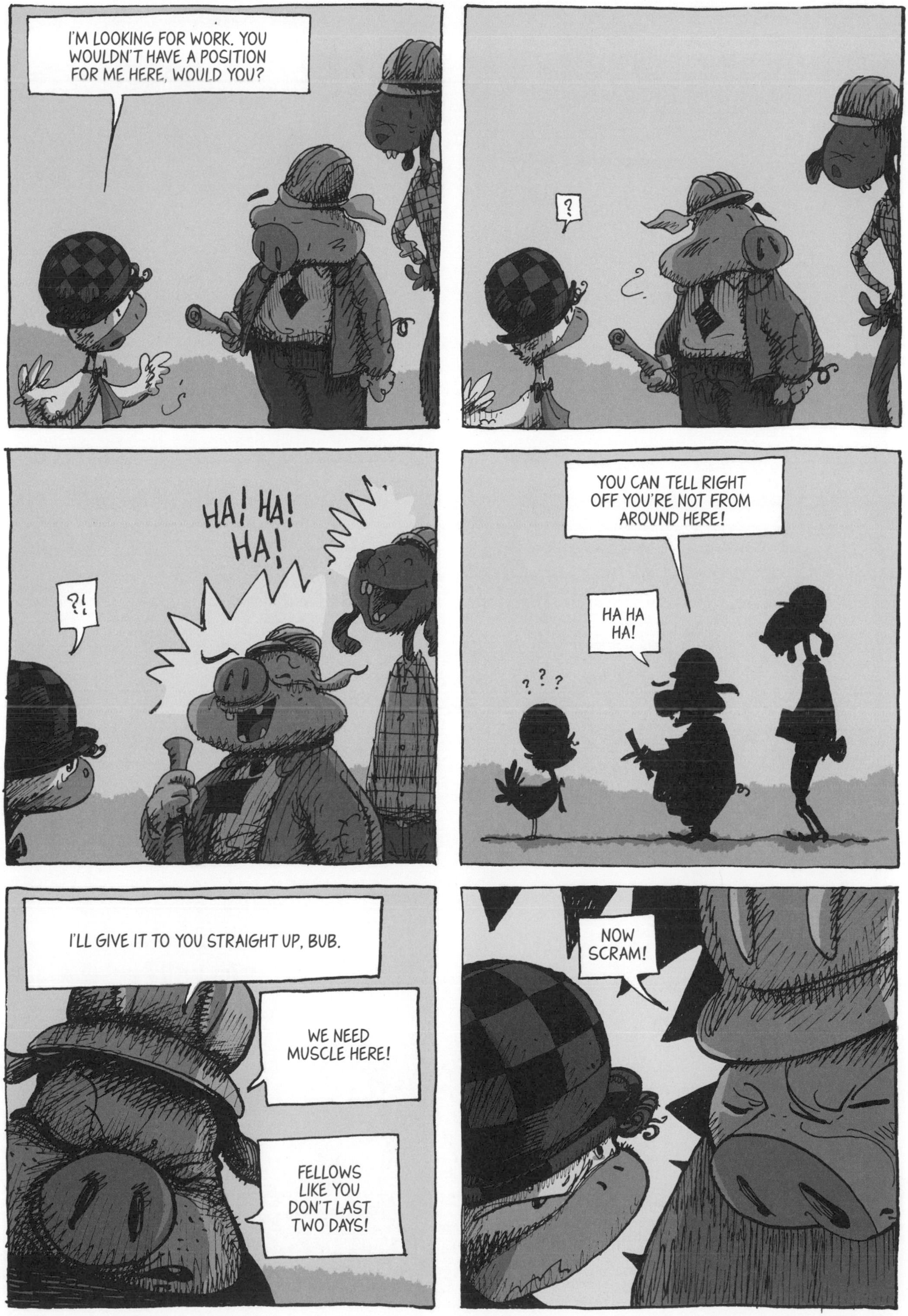
I'M LOOKING FOR WORK. YOU WOULDN'T HAVE A POSITION FOR ME HERE, WOULD YOU?
?
?!
HA! HA! HA!
YOU CAN TELL RIGHT OFF YOU'RE NOT FROM AROUND HERE!
HA HA HA!
? ? ?
I'LL GIVE IT TO YOU STRAIGHT UP, BUB.
WE NEED MUSCLE HERE!
FELLOWS LIKE YOU DON'T LAST TWO DAYS!
NOW SCRAM!

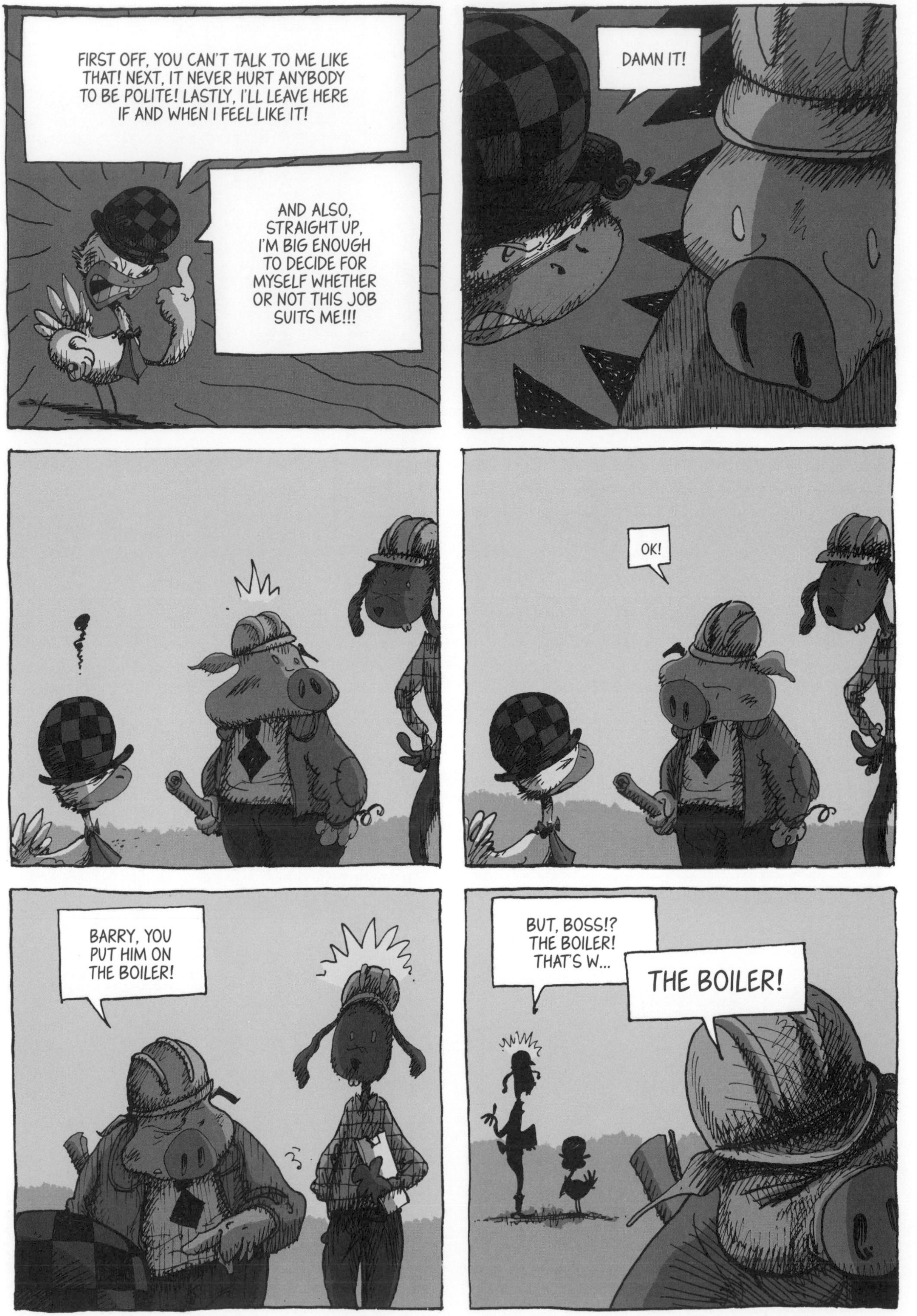
FIRST OFF, YOU CAN'T TALK TO ME LIKE THAT! NEXT, IT NEVER HURT ANYBODY TO BE POLITE! LASTLY, I'LL LEAVE HERE IF AND WHEN I FEEL LIKE IT!
AND ALSO, STRAIGHT UP, I'M BIG ENOUGH TO DECIDE FOR MYSELF WHETHER OR NOT THIS JOB SUITS ME!!!
DAMN IT!
OK!
BARRY, YOU PUT HIM ON THE BOILER!
BUT, BOSS!? THE BOILER! THAT'S W...
THE BOILER!

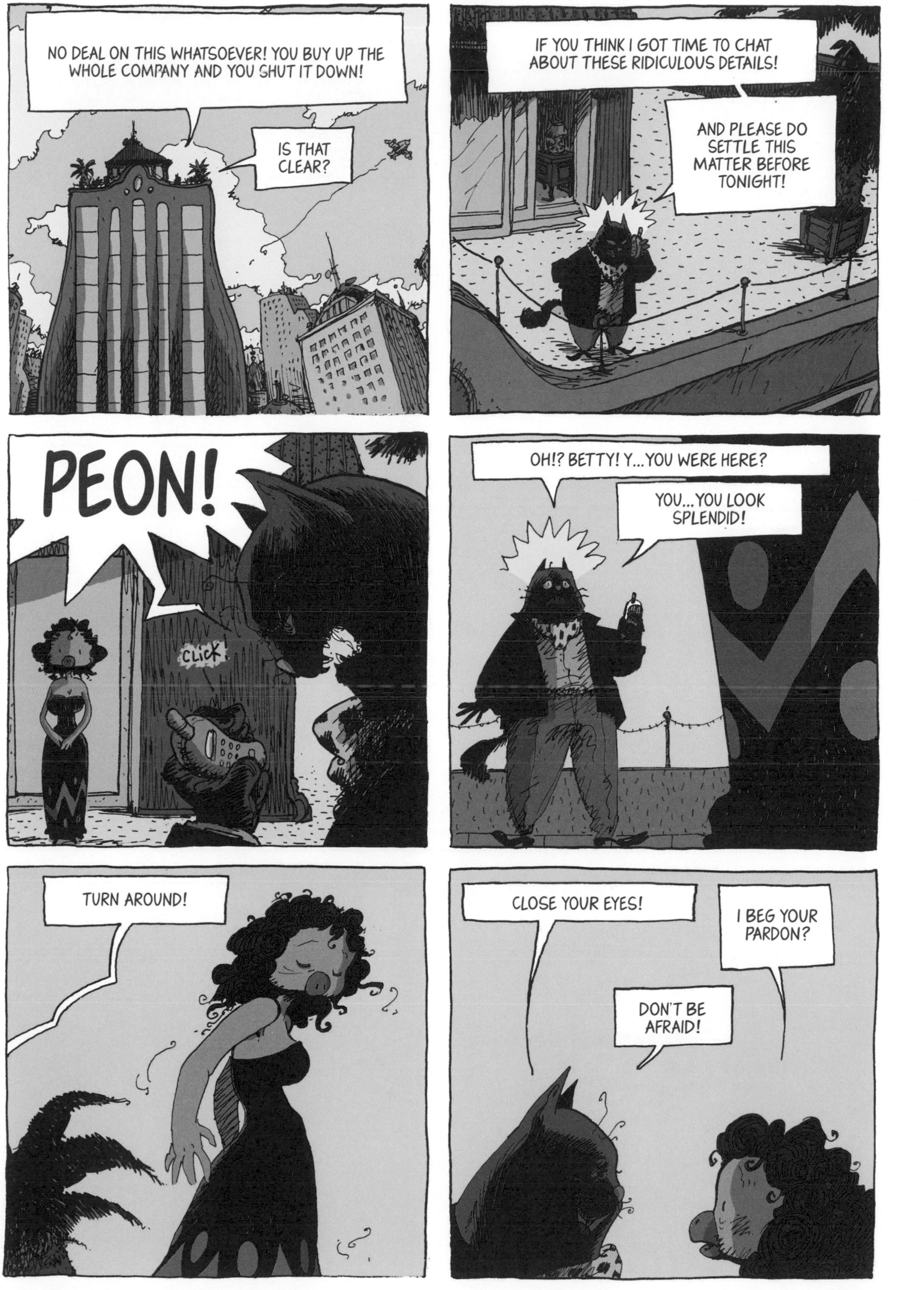
NO DEAL ON THIS WHATSOEVER! YOU BUY UP THE WHOLE COMPANY AND YOU SHUT IT DOWN!
IS THAT CLEAR?
IF YOU THINK I GOT TIME TO CHAT ABOUT THESE RIDICULOUS DETAILS!
AND PLEASE DO SETTLE THIS MATTER BEFORE TONIGHT!
PEON!
CLICK
OH!? BETTY! Y...YOU WERE HERE?
YOU...YOU LOOK SPLENDID!
TURN AROUND!
CLOSE YOUR EYES!
I BEG YOUR PARDON?
DON'T BE AFRAID!

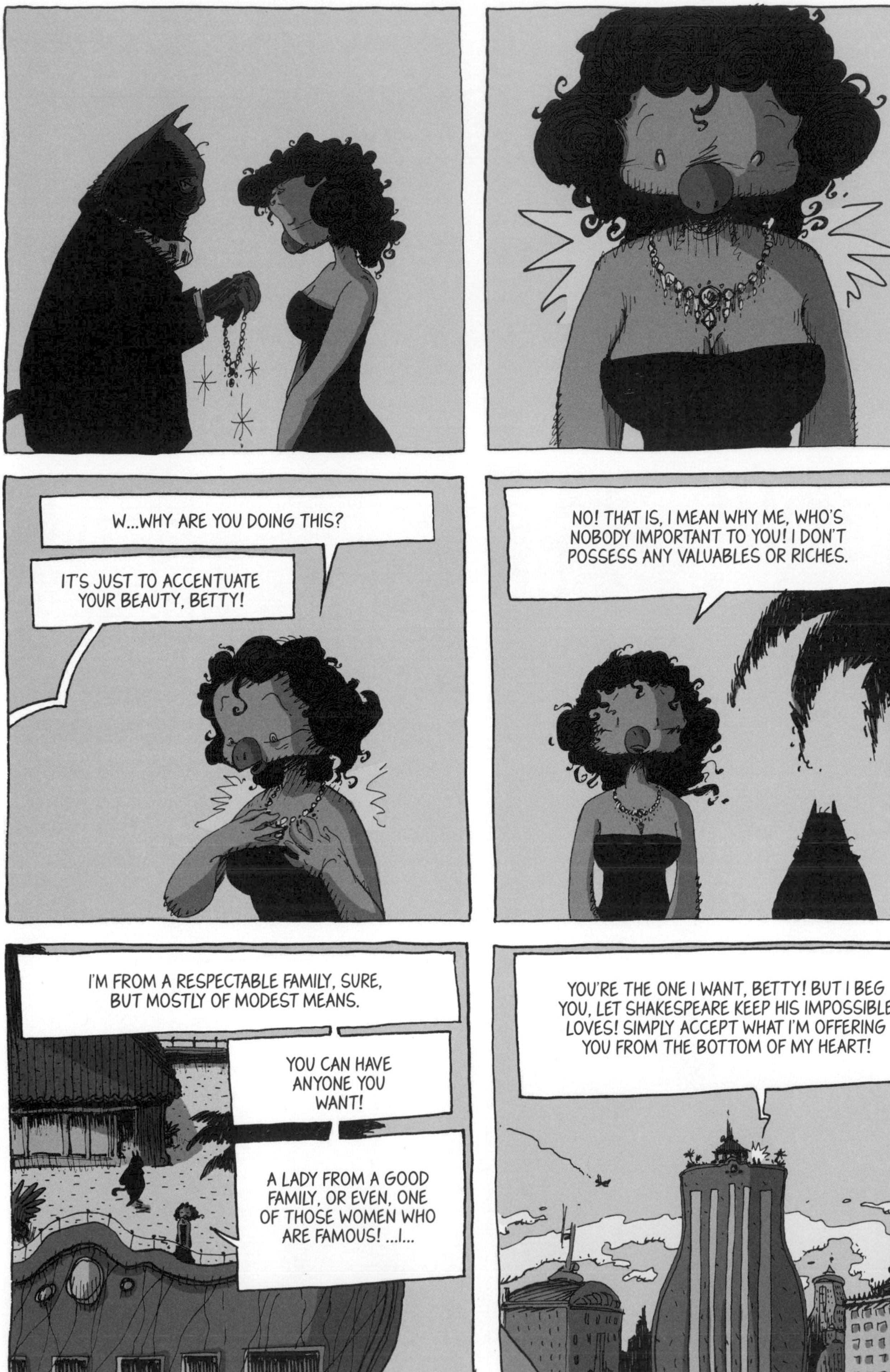
W...WHY ARE YOU DOING THIS?
IT'S JUST TO ACCENTUATE YOUR BEAUTY, BETTY!
NO! THAT IS, I MEAN WHY ME, WHO'S NOBODY IMPORTANT TO YOU! I DON'T POSSESS ANY VALUABLES OR RICHES.
I'M FROM A RESPECTABLE FAMILY, SURE, BUT MOSTLY OF MODEST MEANS.
YOU CAN HAVE ANYONE YOU WANT!
A LADY FROM A GOOD FAMILY, OR EVEN, ONE OF THOSE WOMEN WHO ARE FAMOUS! ...I...
YOU'RE THE ONE I WANT, BETTY! BUT I BEG YOU, LET SHAKESPEARE KEEP HIS IMPOSSIBLE LOVES! SIMPLY ACCEPT WHAT I'M OFFERING YOU FROM THE BOTTOM OF MY HEART!

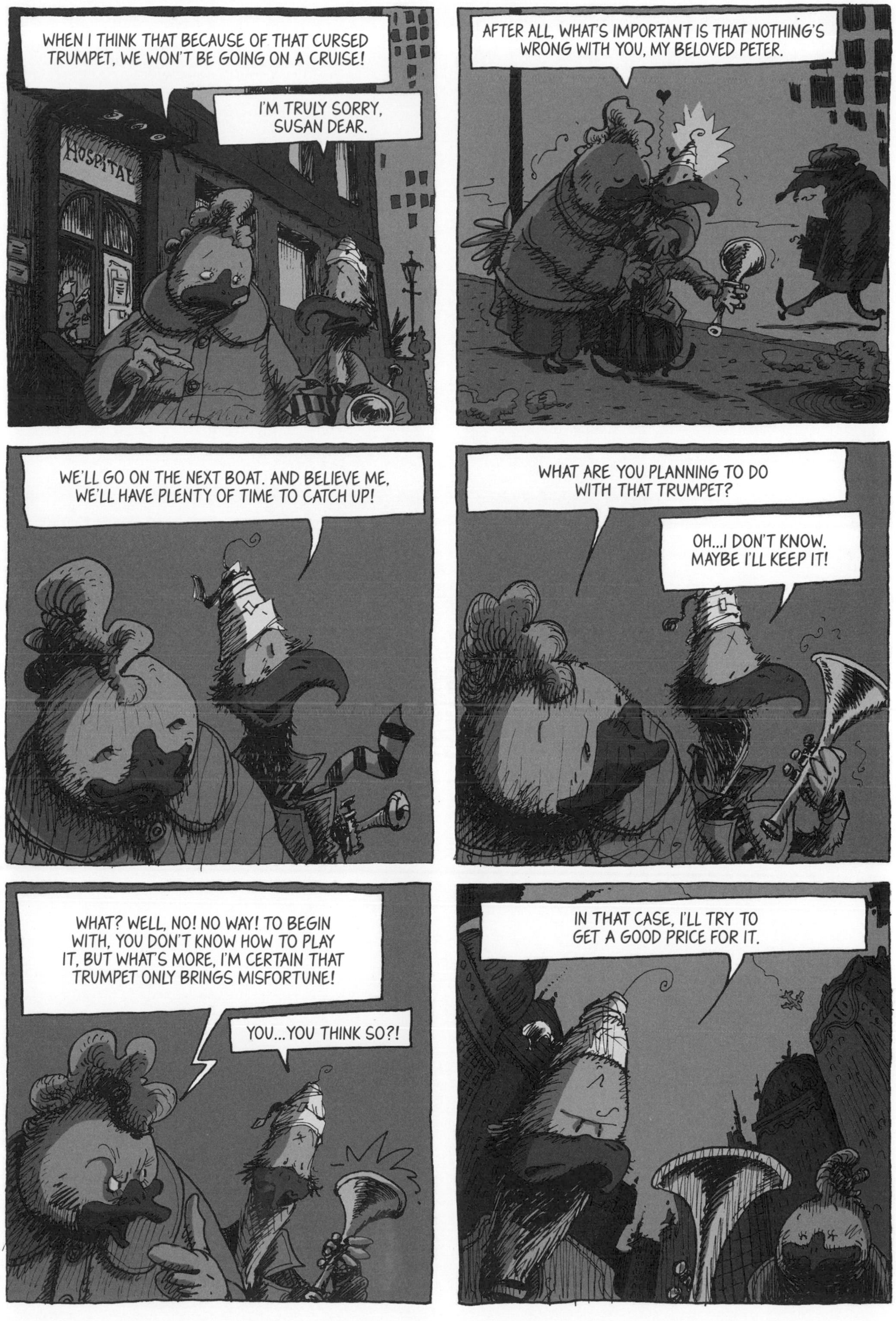
WHEN I THINK THAT BECAUSE OF THAT CURSED TRUMPET, WE WON'T BE GOING ON A CRUISE!
I'M TRULY SORRY, SUSAN DEAR.
HOSPITAL
AFTER ALL, WHAT'S IMPORTANT IS THAT NOTHING'S WRONG WITH YOU, MY BELOVED PETER.
WE'LL GO ON THE NEXT BOAT. AND BELIEVE ME, WE'LL HAVE PLENTY OF TIME TO CATCH UP!
WHAT ARE YOU PLANNING TO DO WITH THAT TRUMPET?
OH...I DON'T KNOW. MAYBE I'LL KEEP IT!
WHAT? WELL, NO! NO WAY! TO BEGIN WITH, YOU DON'T KNOW HOW TO PLAY IT, BUT WHAT'S MORE, I'M CERTAIN THAT TRUMPET ONLY BRINGS MISFORTUNE!
YOU...YOU THINK SO?!
IN THAT CASE, I'LL TRY TO GET A GOOD PRICE FOR IT.

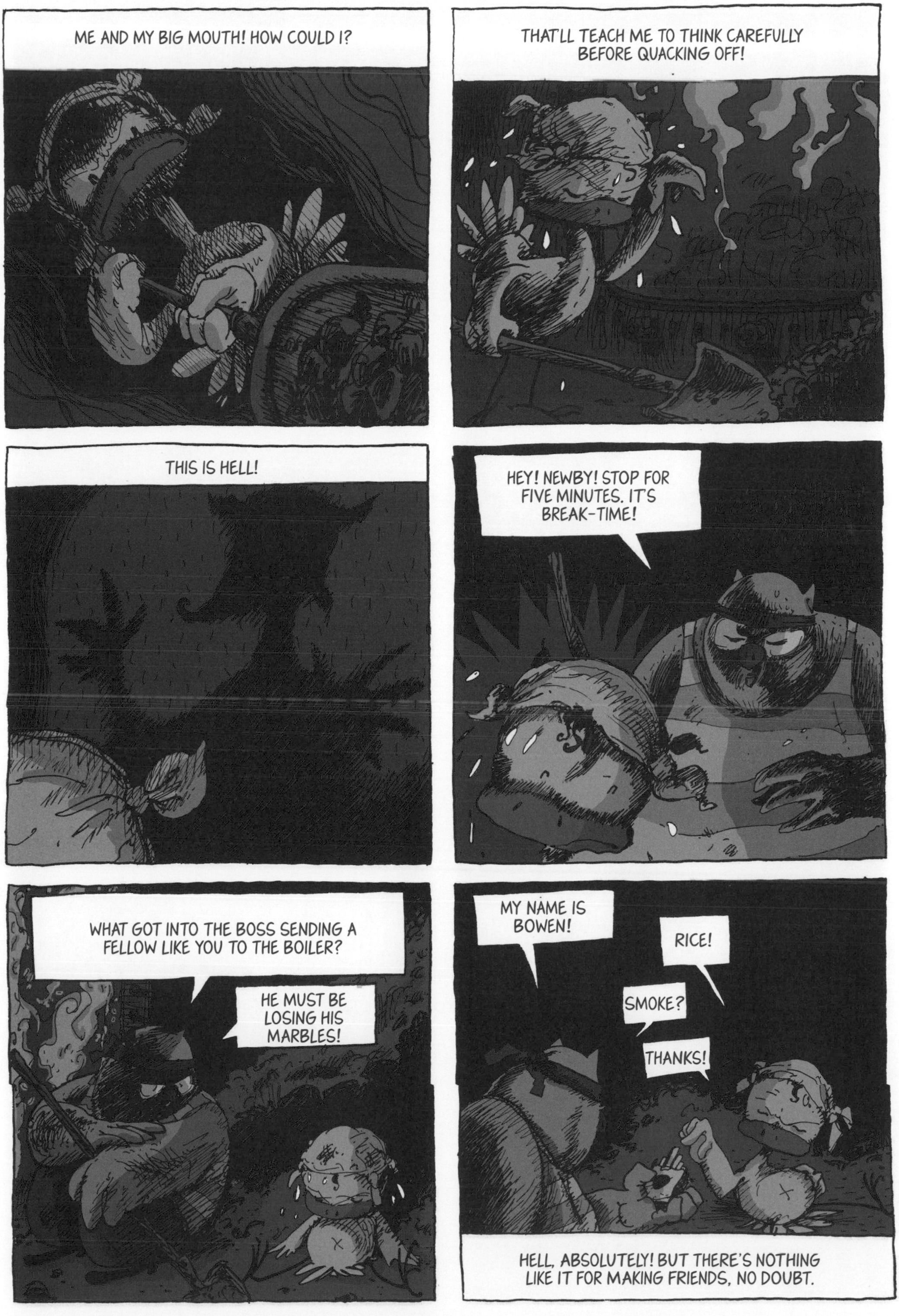

ME AND MY BIG MOUTH! HOW COULD I?
THAT'LL TEACH ME TO THINK CAREFULLY BEFORE QUACKING OFF!
THIS IS HELL!
HEY! NEWBY! STOP FOR FIVE MINUTES. IT'S BREAK-TIME!
WHAT GOT INTO THE BOSS SENDING A FELLOW LIKE YOU TO THE BOILER?
HE MUST BE LOSING HIS MARBLES!
MY NAME IS BOWEN!
RICE!
SMOKE?
THANKS!
HELL, ABSOLUTELY! BUT THERE'S NOTHING LIKE IT FOR MAKING FRIENDS, NO DOUBT.

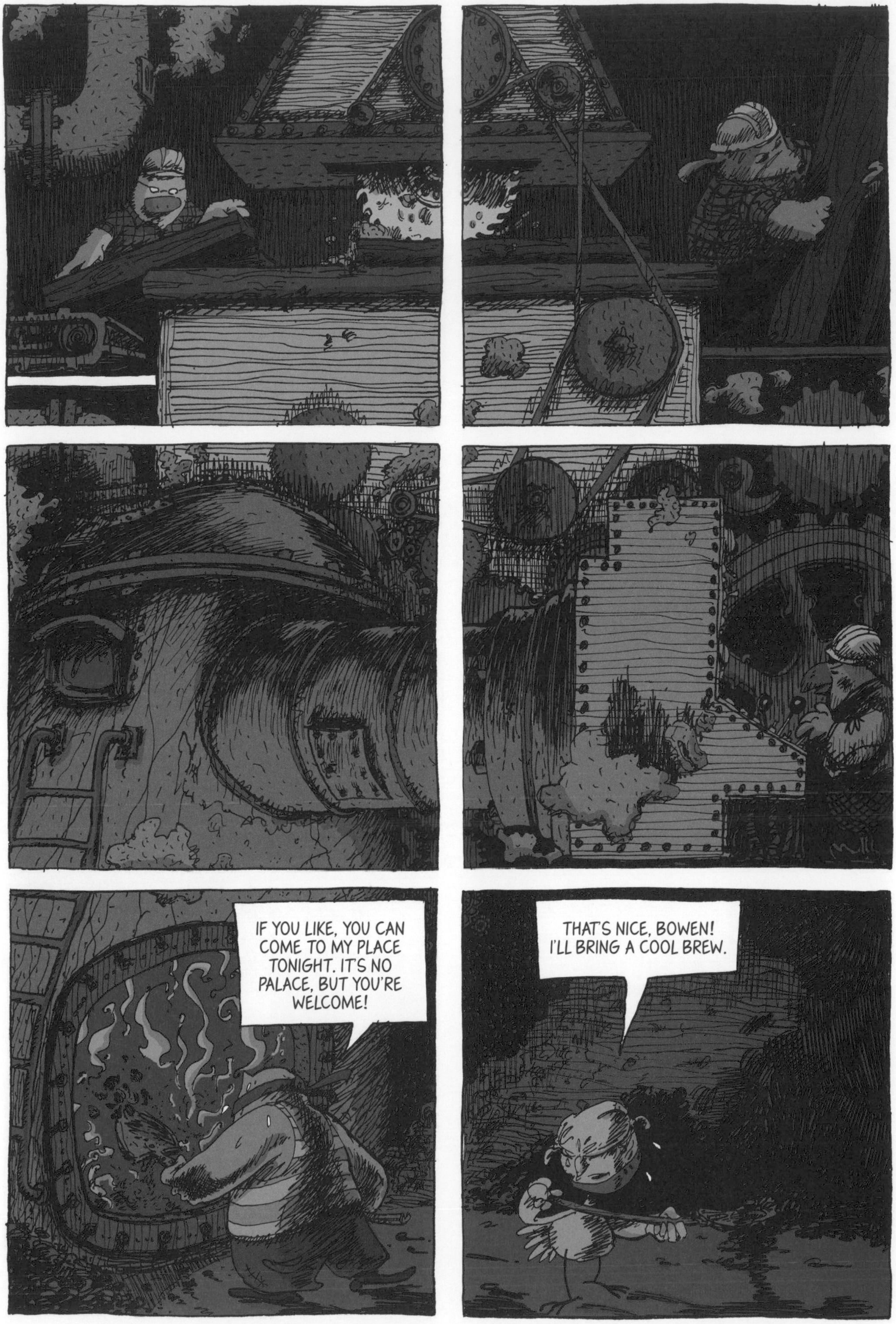
IF YOU LIKE, YOU CAN COME TO MY PLACE TONIGHT. IT'S NO PALACE, BUT YOU'RE WELCOME!
THAT'S NICE, BOWEN! I'LL BRING A COOL BREW.

I HAD NO DESIRE TO DIG UP MY PAST...THAT'S WHY I DECIDED TO INVENT ONE FOR MYSELF.

THERE'S MY LITTLE HOME!

OH, NOT AN EXCEPTIONAL PAST. JUST SOMETHING TO KEEP FROM TALKING TO HIM ABOUT BETTY, ABOUT JAZZ.

YOU CAN CRASH HERE TILL YOU FIND YOURSELF A PLACE.

THANKS, I DON'T...

YOU CAN LIE TO OTHERS, BUT NOT TO YOURSELF! TRY TO FLEE REALITY, AND SOMETIMES, IT'LL BLOW UP RIGHT IN YOUR FACE!

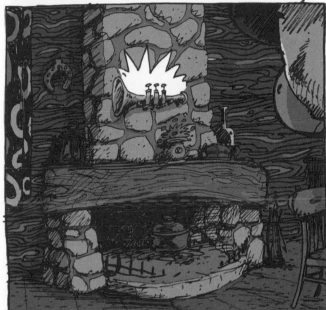

SOMETHING WRONG, RICE?

RICE!?

WHAT? UH, NO, IT'S ALL GOOD. JUST A LITTLE TIRED.

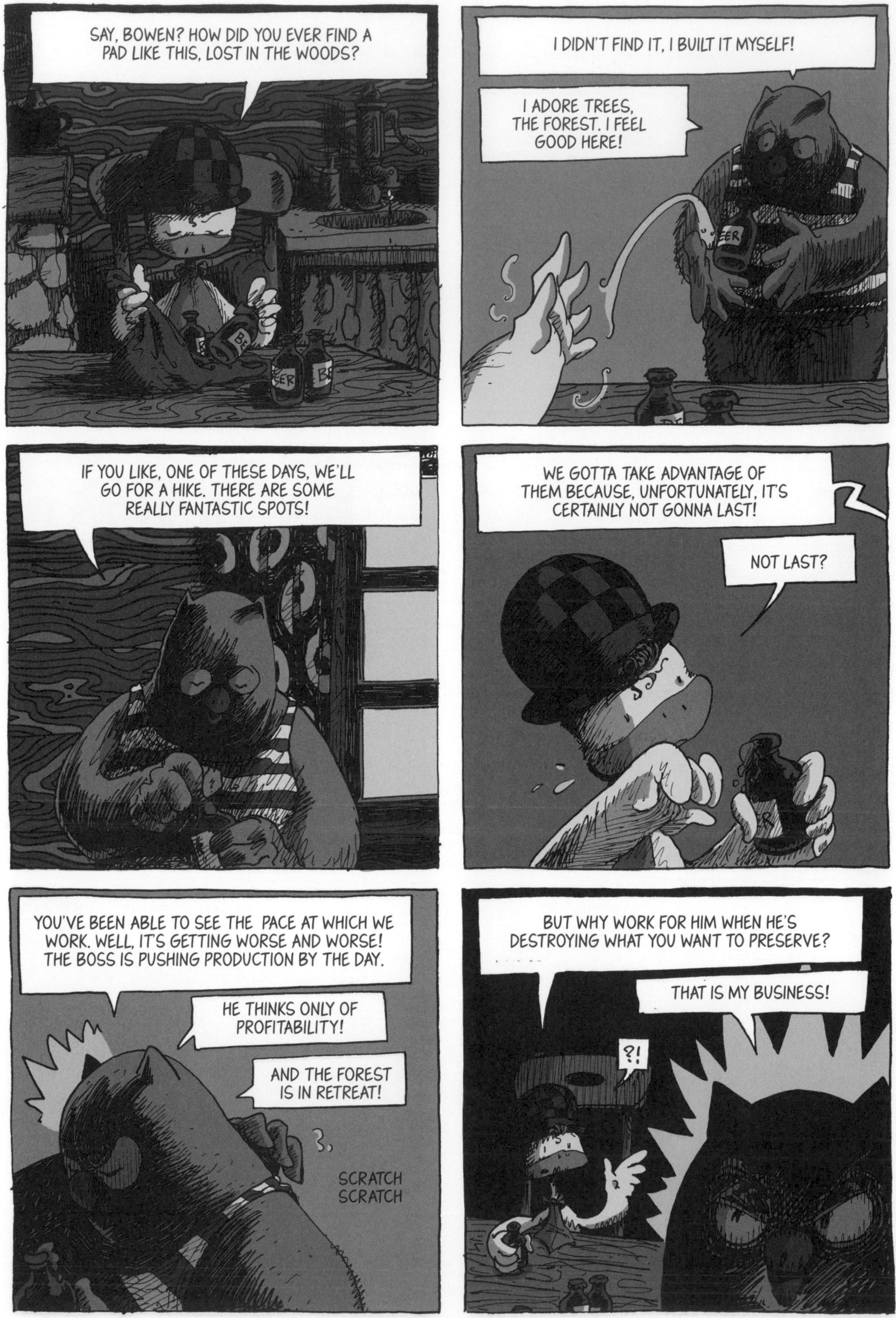

SAY, BOWEN? HOW DID YOU EVER FIND A PAD LIKE THIS, LOST IN THE WOODS?
I DIDN'T FIND IT, I BUILT IT MYSELF!
I ADORE TREES, THE FOREST. I FEEL GOOD HERE!
IF YOU LIKE, ONE OF THESE DAYS, WE'LL GO FOR A HIKE. THERE ARE SOME REALLY FANTASTIC SPOTS!
WE GOTTA TAKE ADVANTAGE OF THEM BECAUSE, UNFORTUNATELY, IT'S CERTAINLY NOT GONNA LAST!
NOT LAST?
YOU'VE BEEN ABLE TO SEE THE PACE AT WHICH WE WORK. WELL, IT'S GETTING WORSE AND WORSE! THE BOSS IS PUSHING PRODUCTION BY THE DAY.
HE THINKS ONLY OF PROFITABILITY!
AND THE FOREST IS IN RETREAT!
SCRATCH SCRATCH
BUT WHY WORK FOR HIM WHEN HE'S DESTROYING WHAT YOU WANT TO PRESERVE?
THAT IS MY BUSINESS!
?!

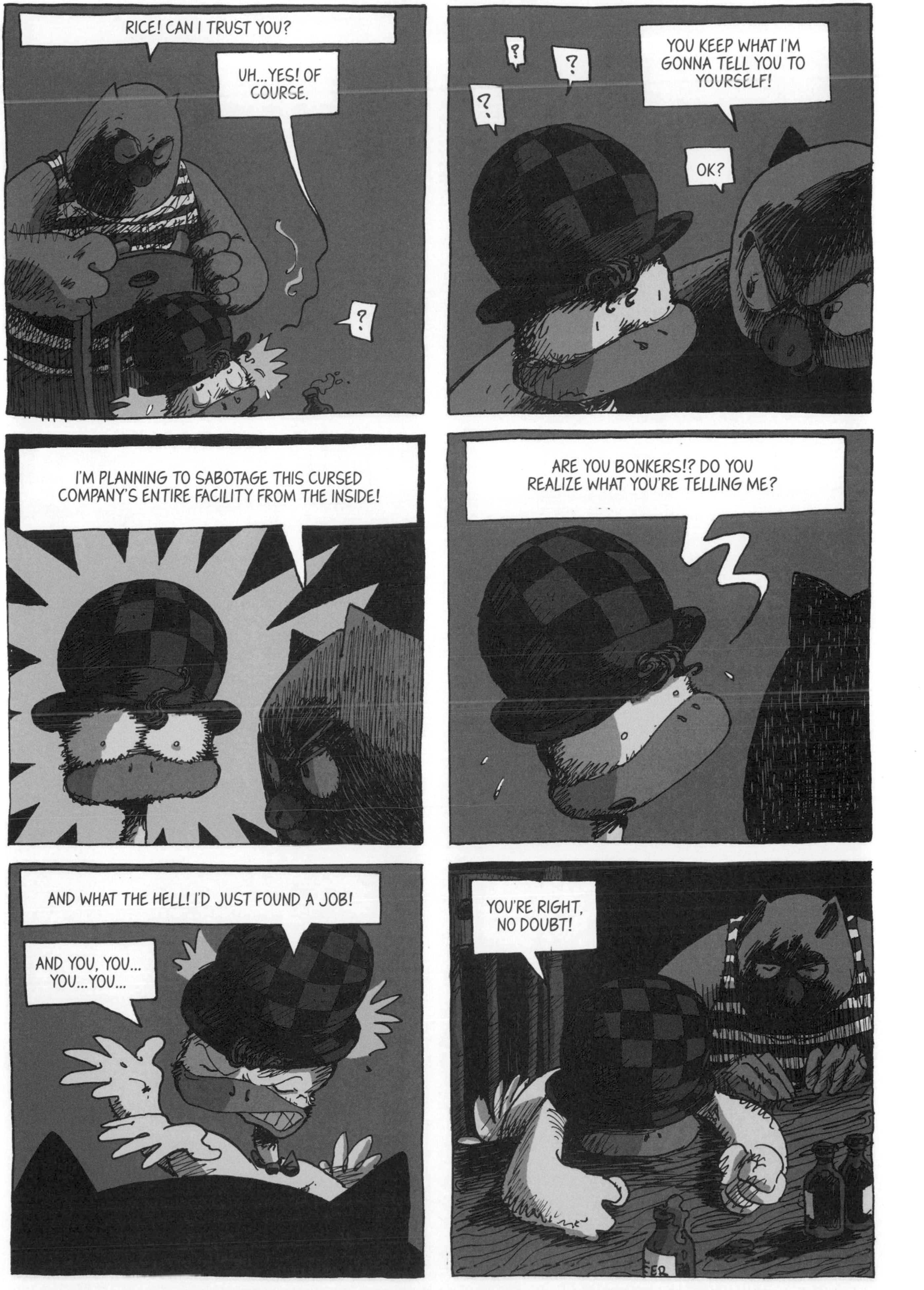

RICE! CAN I TRUST YOU?
UH...YES! OF COURSE.
?
?
?
?
YOU KEEP WHAT I'M GONNA TELL YOU TO YOURSELF!
OK?
I'M PLANNING TO SABOTAGE THIS CURSED COMPANY'S ENTIRE FACILITY FROM THE INSIDE!
ARE YOU BONKERS!? DO YOU REALIZE WHAT YOU'RE TELLING ME?
AND WHAT THE HELL! I'D JUST FOUND A JOB!
AND YOU, YOU... YOU...YOU...
YOU'RE RIGHT, NO DOUBT!

WHAT MESS HAD I STUMBLED INTO!?

GOODNIGHT, RICE!

GOODNIGHT, BOWEN!

HERE I WAS IN THE HOME OF AN OWL WITH A HEART OF GOLD, CERTAINLY, BUT MY BUDDY JUST HAD TO TURN OUT TO BE A TERRORIST!

AND TO TOP IT OFF, HE HAD TO PUT MY MATTRESS DOWN RIGHT IN FRONT OF THE FIREPLACE.

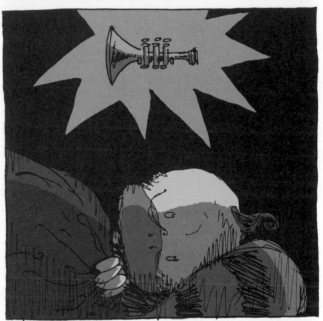

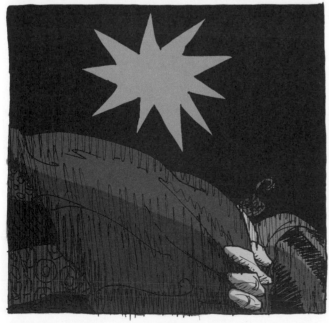

BETTY...

44

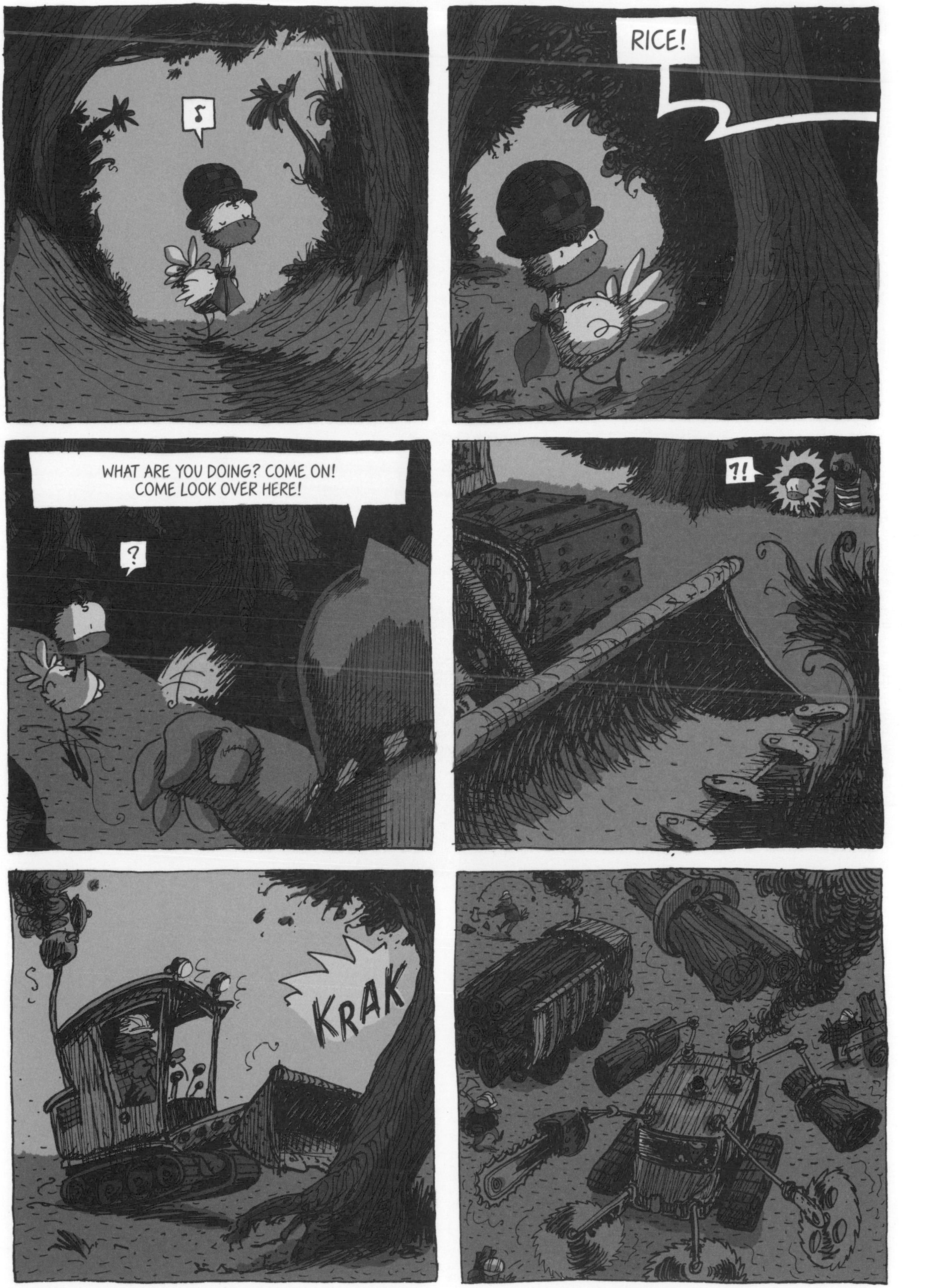

RICE!
WHAT ARE YOU DOING? COME ON! COME LOOK OVER HERE!
?
?!
KRAK

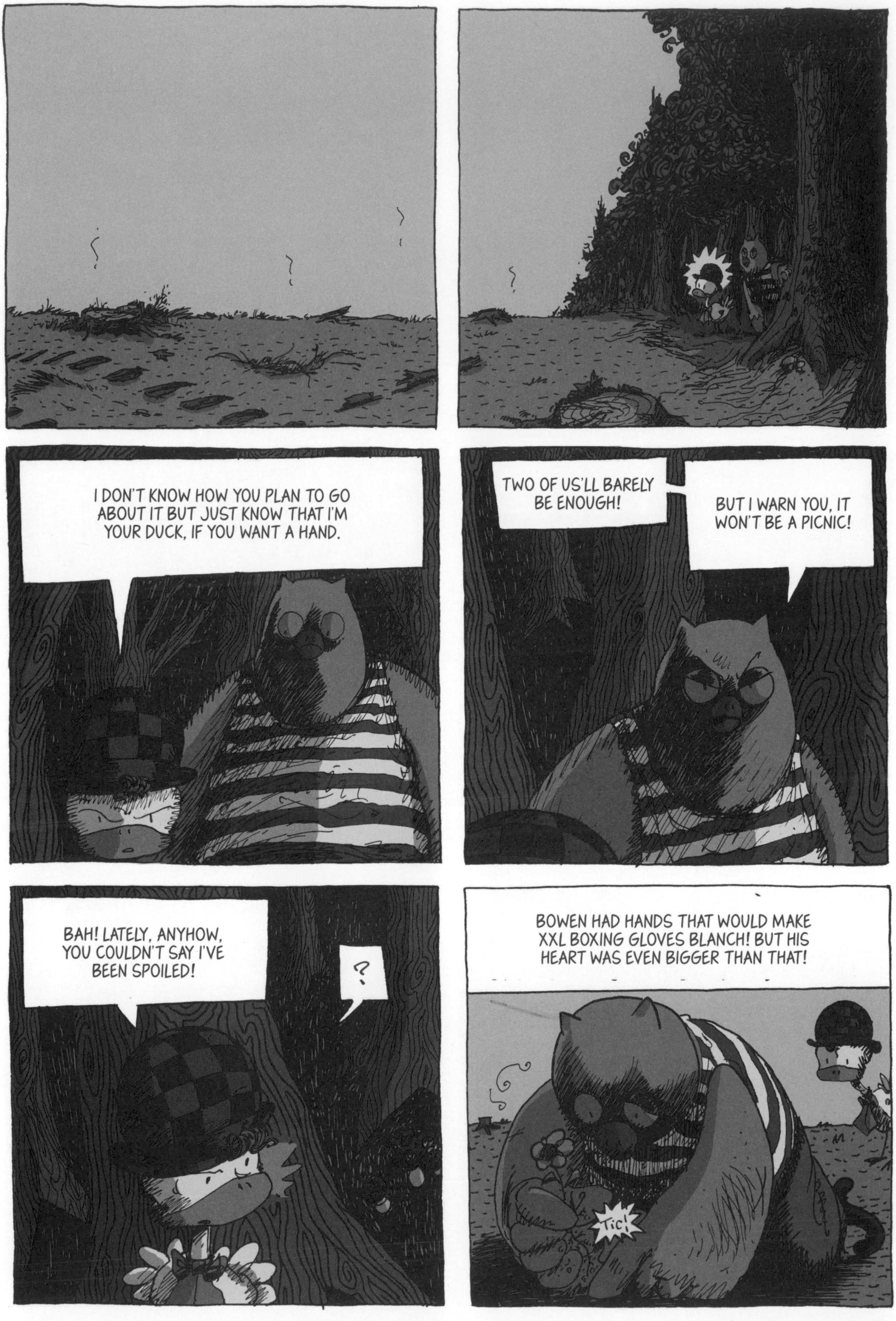
I DON'T KNOW HOW YOU PLAN TO GO ABOUT IT BUT JUST KNOW THAT I'M YOUR DUCK, IF YOU WANT A HAND.
TWO OF US'LL BARELY BE ENOUGH!
BUT I WARN YOU, IT WON'T BE A PICNIC!
BAH! LATELY, ANYHOW, YOU COULDN'T SAY I'VE BEEN SPOILED!
?
BOWEN HAD HANDS THAT WOULD MAKE XXL BOXING GLOVES BLANCH! BUT HIS HEART WAS EVEN BIGGER THAN THAT!
TIC!

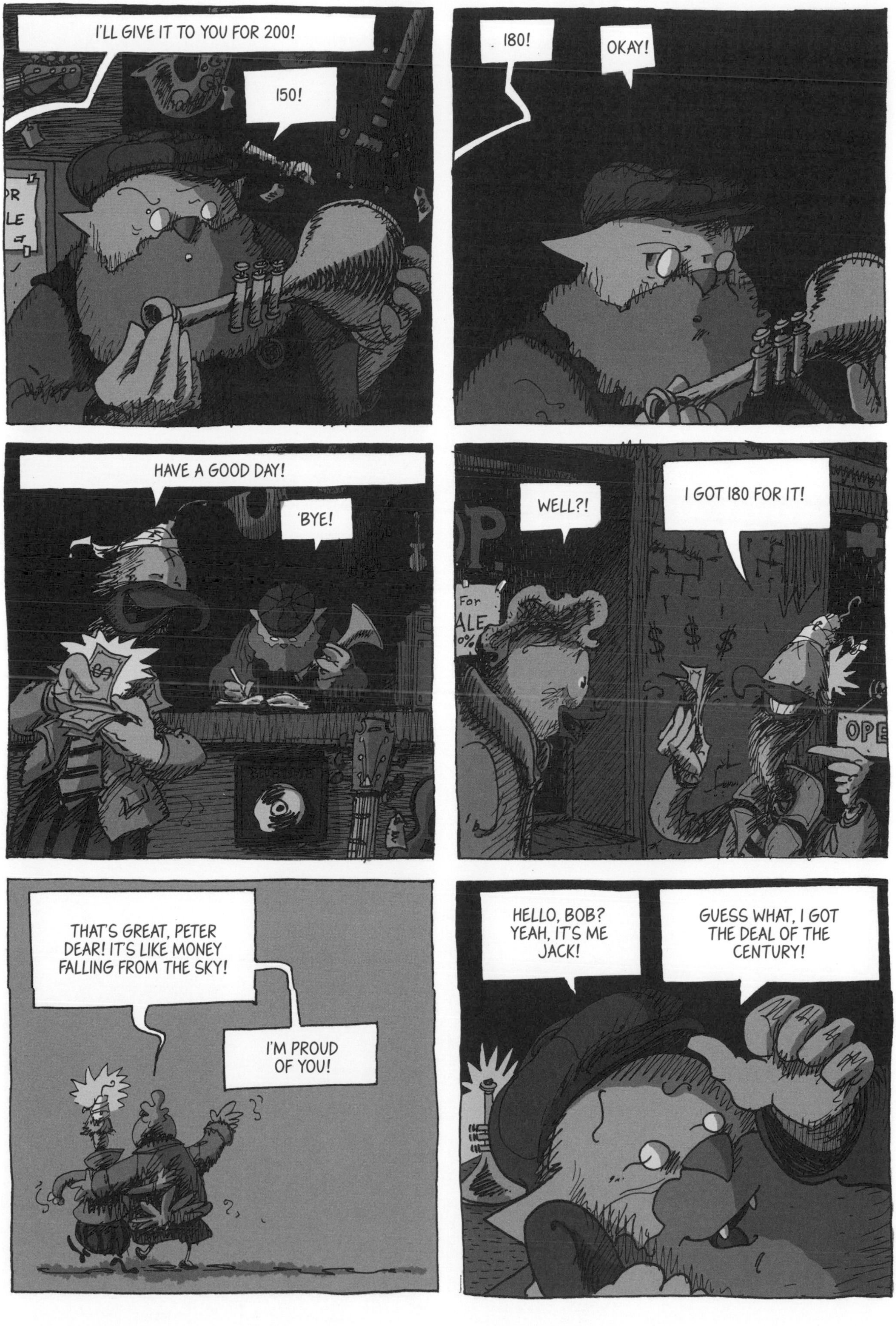
I'LL GIVE IT TO YOU FOR 200!
150!
180!
OKAY!
HAVE A GOOD DAY!
'BYE!
WELL?!
I GOT 180 FOR IT!
THAT'S GREAT, PETER DEAR! IT'S LIKE MONEY FALLING FROM THE SKY!
I'M PROUD OF YOU!
HELLO, BOB? YEAH, IT'S ME JACK!
GUESS WHAT, I GOT THE DEAL OF THE CENTURY!

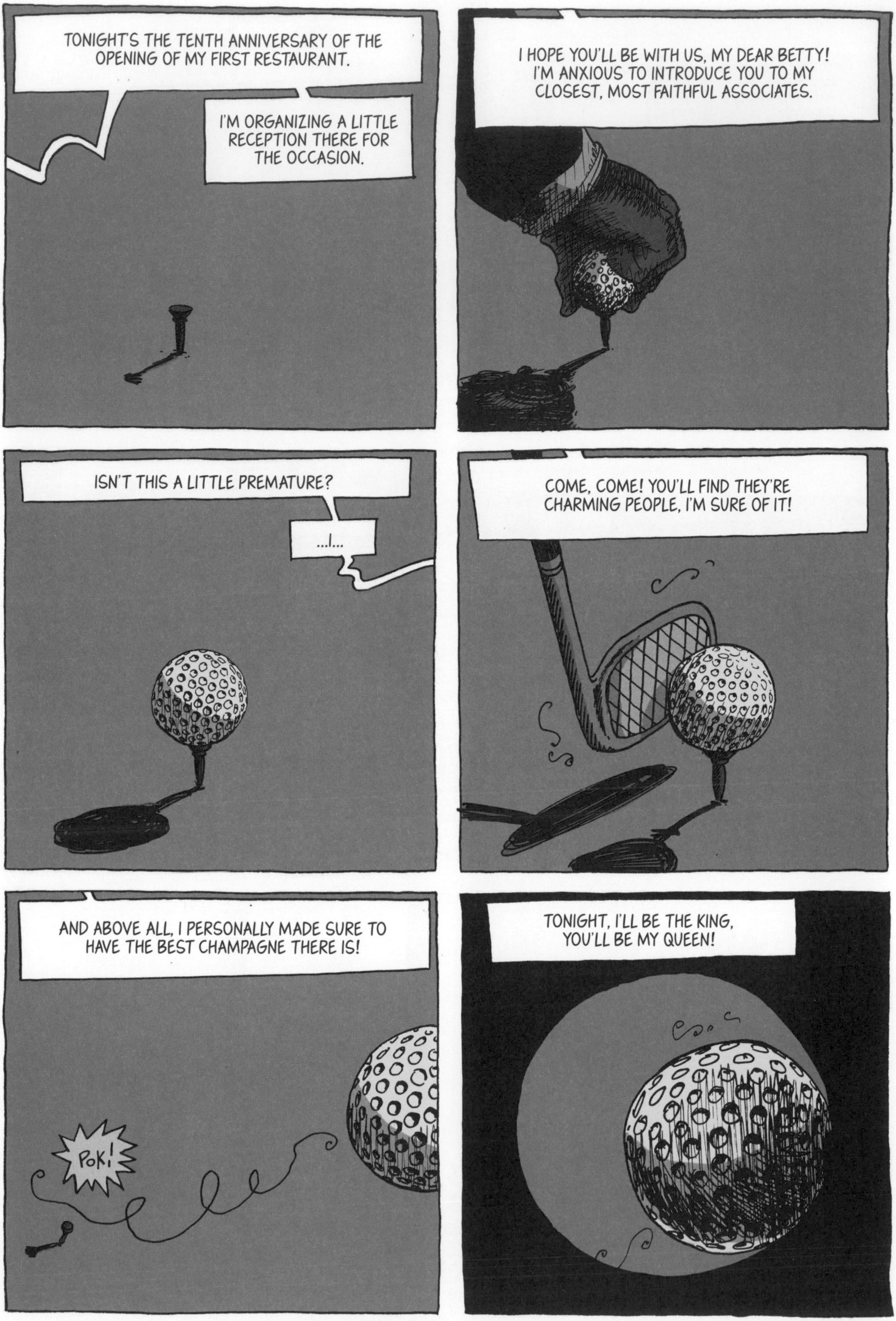
TONIGHT'S THE TENTH ANNIVERSARY OF THE OPENING OF MY FIRST RESTAURANT.
I'M ORGANIZING A LITTLE RECEPTION THERE FOR THE OCCASION.
I HOPE YOU'LL BE WITH US, MY DEAR BETTY! I'M ANXIOUS TO INTRODUCE YOU TO MY CLOSEST, MOST FAITHFUL ASSOCIATES.
ISN'T THIS A LITTLE PREMATURE?
...I...
COME, COME! YOU'LL FIND THEY'RE CHARMING PEOPLE, I'M SURE OF IT!
AND ABOVE ALL, I PERSONALLY MADE SURE TO HAVE THE BEST CHAMPAGNE THERE IS!
POK!
TONIGHT, I'LL BE THE KING, YOU'LL BE MY QUEEN!

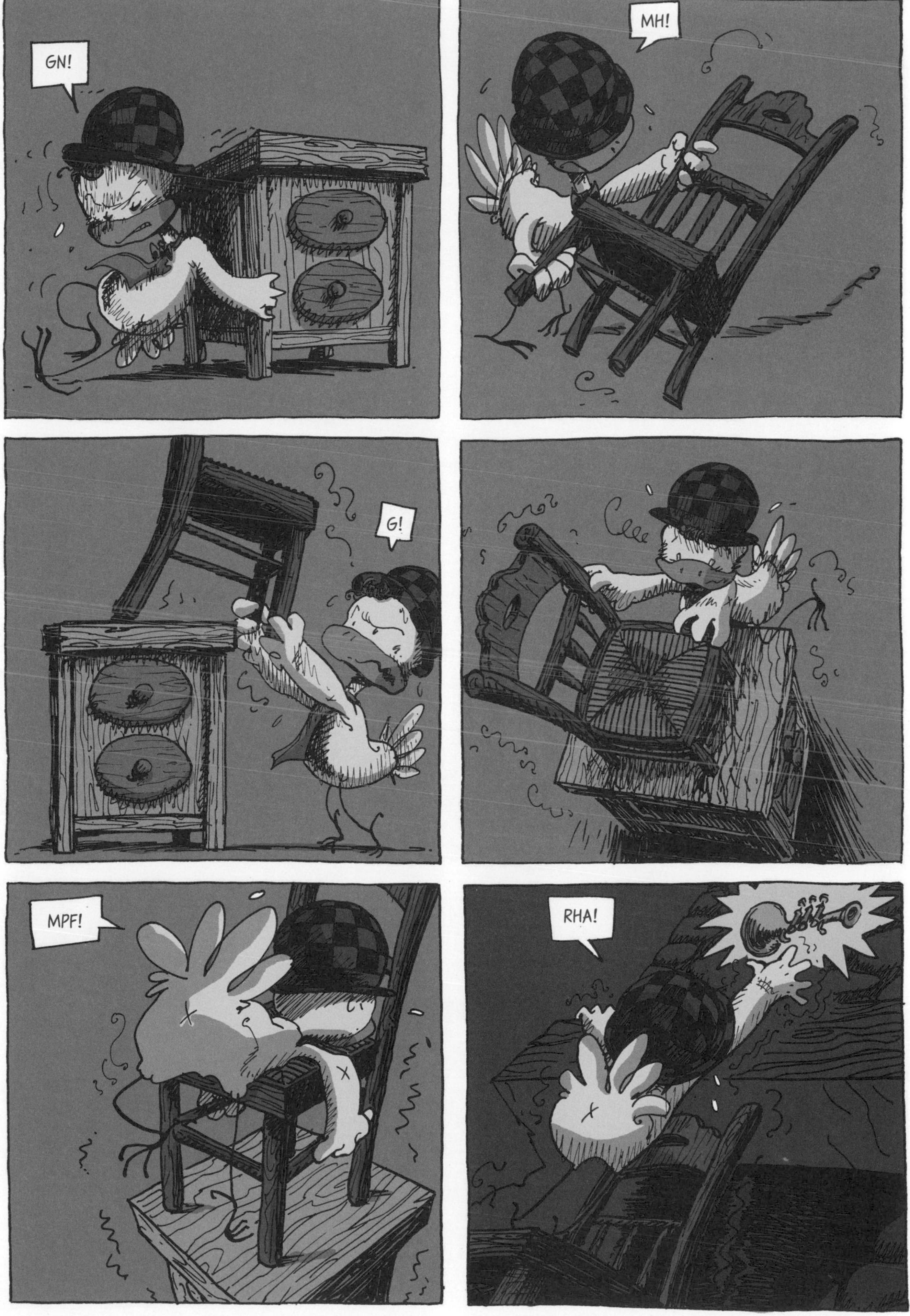
GN!
MH!
G!
MPF!
RHA!

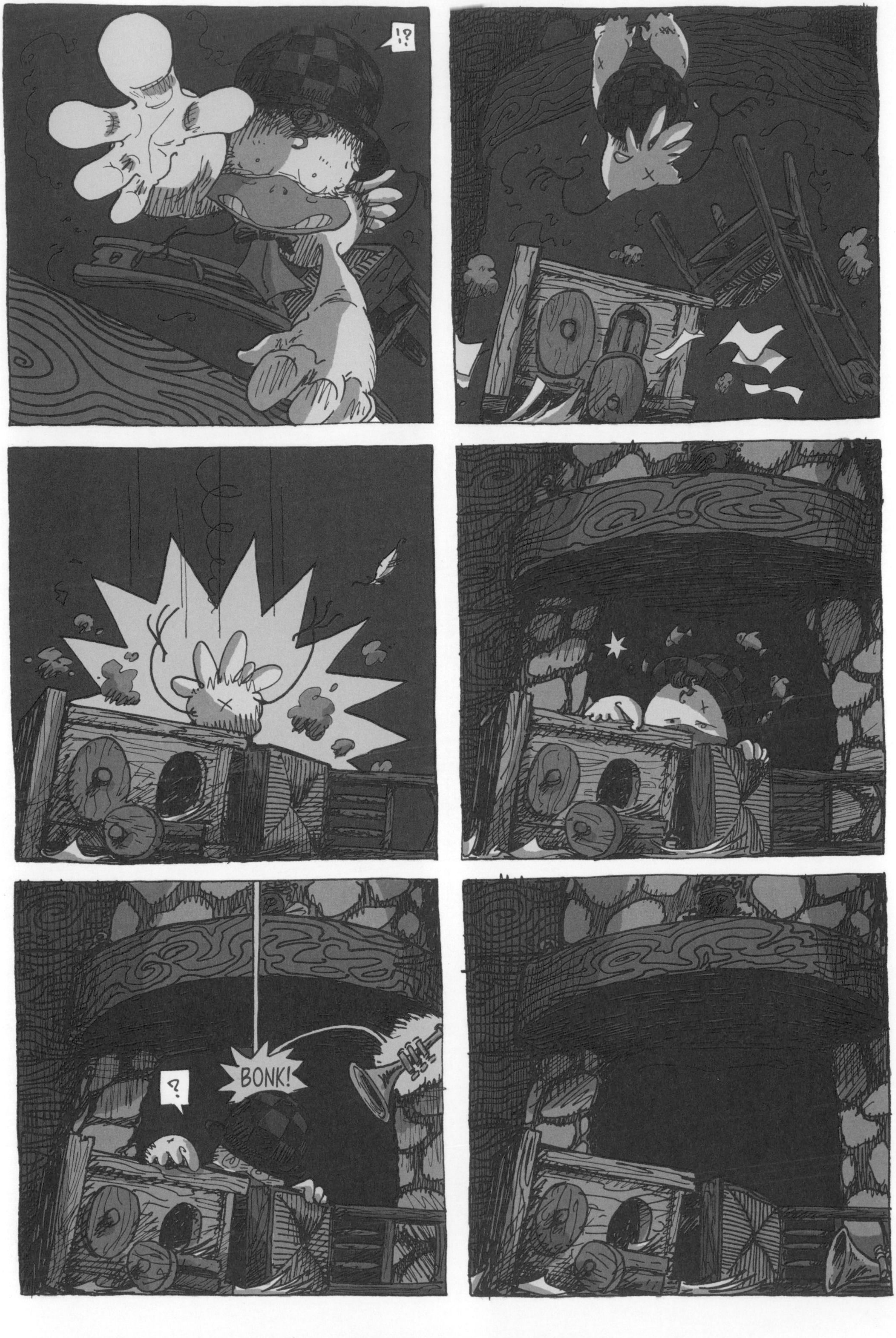
!?
?
BONK!

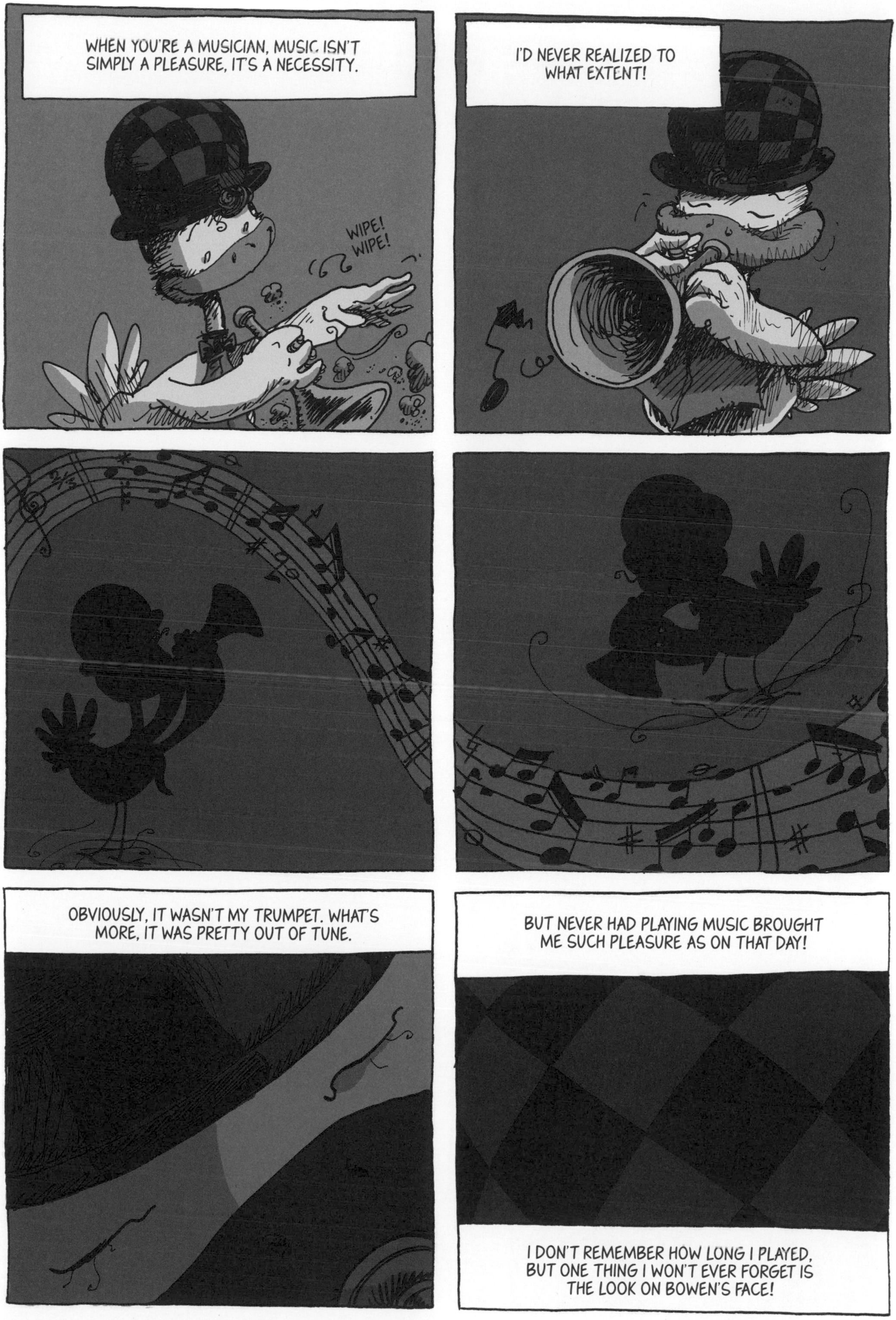
WHEN YOU'RE A MUSICIAN, MUSIC ISN'T SIMPLY A PLEASURE, IT'S A NECESSITY.
WIPE! WIPE!
I'D NEVER REALIZED TO WHAT EXTENT!
OBVIOUSLY, IT WASN'T MY TRUMPET. WHAT'S MORE, IT WAS PRETTY OUT OF TUNE.
BUT NEVER HAD PLAYING MUSIC BROUGHT ME SUCH PLEASURE AS ON THAT DAY!
I DON'T REMEMBER HOW LONG I PLAYED, BUT ONE THING I WON'T EVER FORGET IS THE LOOK ON BOWEN'S FACE!

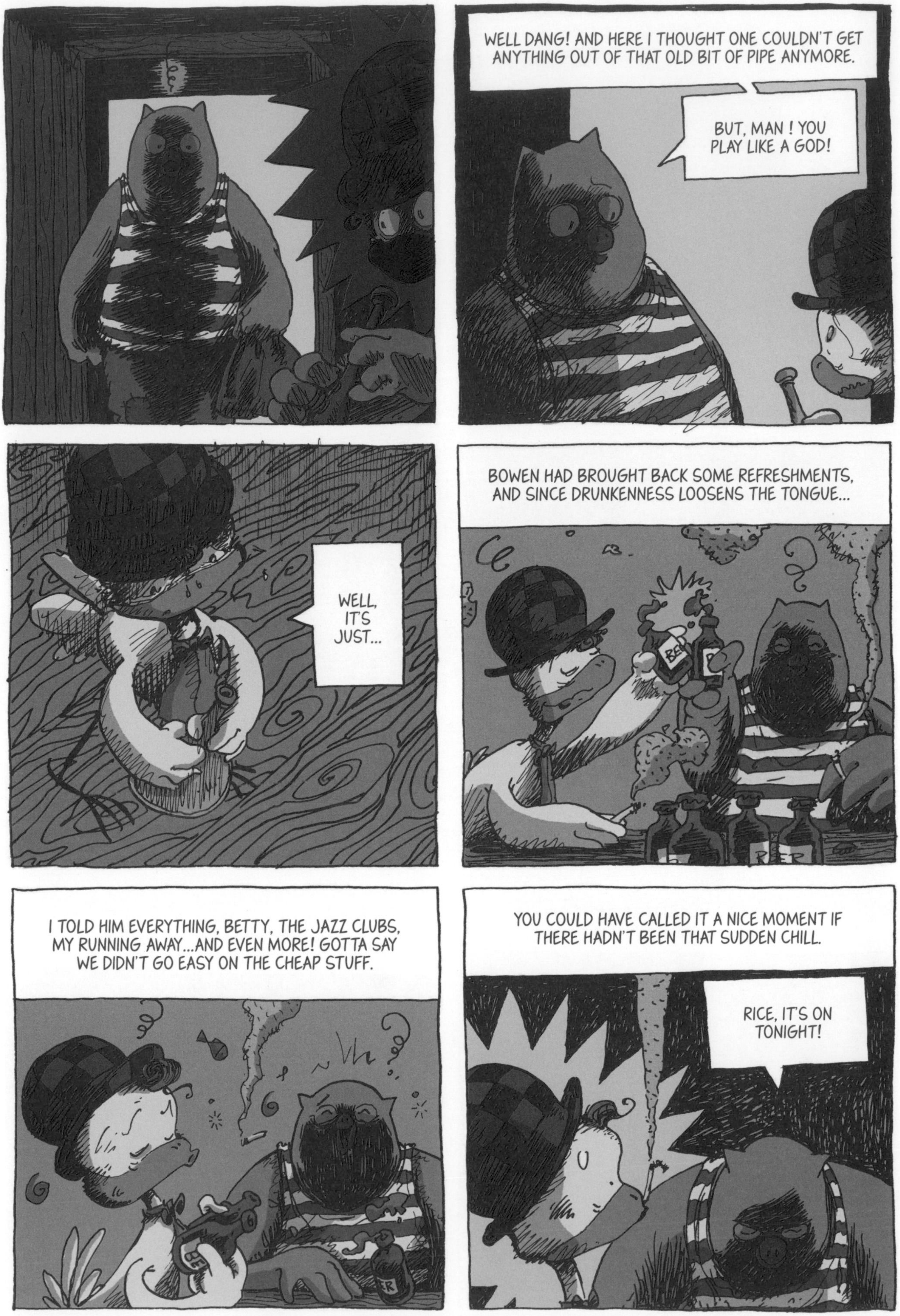
WELL DANG! AND HERE I THOUGHT ONE COULDN'T GET ANYTHING OUT OF THAT OLD BIT OF PIPE ANYMORE.
BUT, MAN ! YOU PLAY LIKE A GOD!
WELL, IT'S JUST...
BOWEN HAD BROUGHT BACK SOME REFRESHMENTS, AND SINCE DRUNKENNESS LOOSENS THE TONGUE...
I TOLD HIM EVERYTHING, BETTY, THE JAZZ CLUBS, MY RUNNING AWAY...AND EVEN MORE! GOTTA SAY WE DIDN'T GO EASY ON THE CHEAP STUFF.
YOU COULD HAVE CALLED IT A NICE MOMENT IF THERE HADN'T BEEN THAT SUDDEN CHILL.
RICE, IT'S ON TONIGHT!

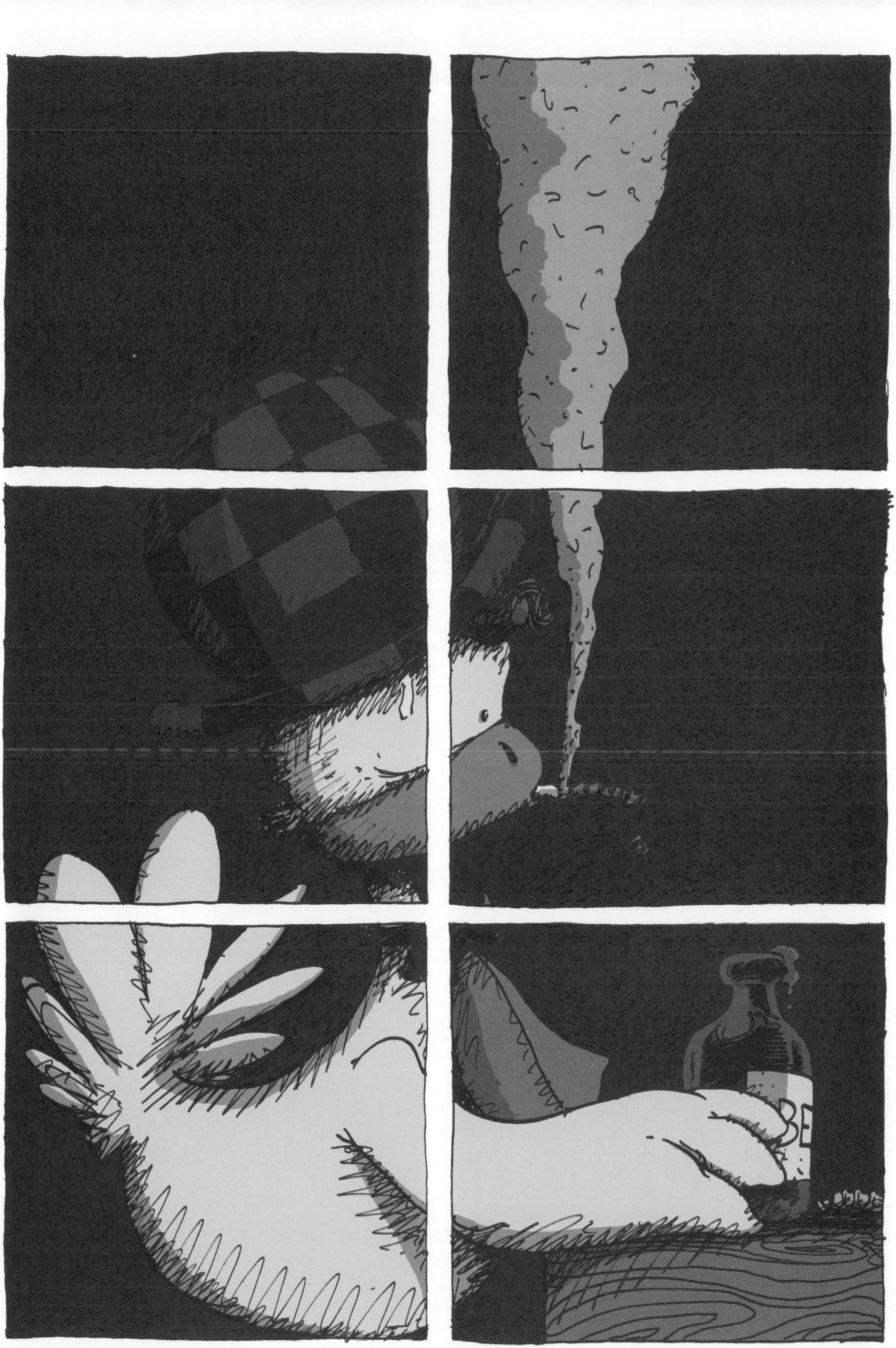

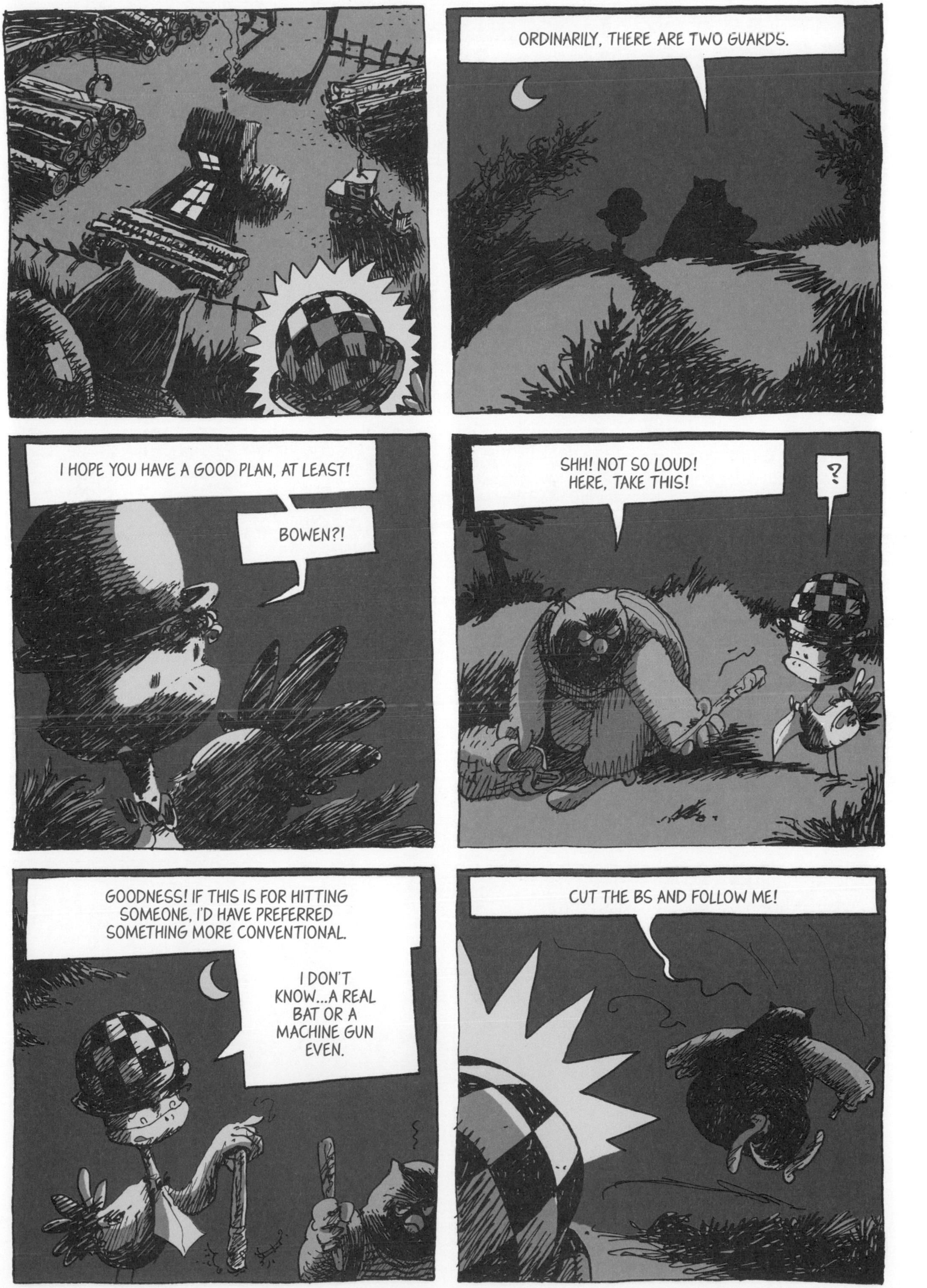
ORDINARILY, THERE ARE TWO GUARDS.
I HOPE YOU HAVE A GOOD PLAN, AT LEAST!
BOWEN?!
SHH! NOT SO LOUD! HERE, TAKE THIS!
?
GOODNESS! IF THIS IS FOR HITTING SOMEONE, I'D HAVE PREFERRED SOMETHING MORE CONVENTIONAL.
I DON'T KNOW...A REAL BAT OR A MACHINE GUN EVEN.
CUT THE BS AND FOLLOW ME!

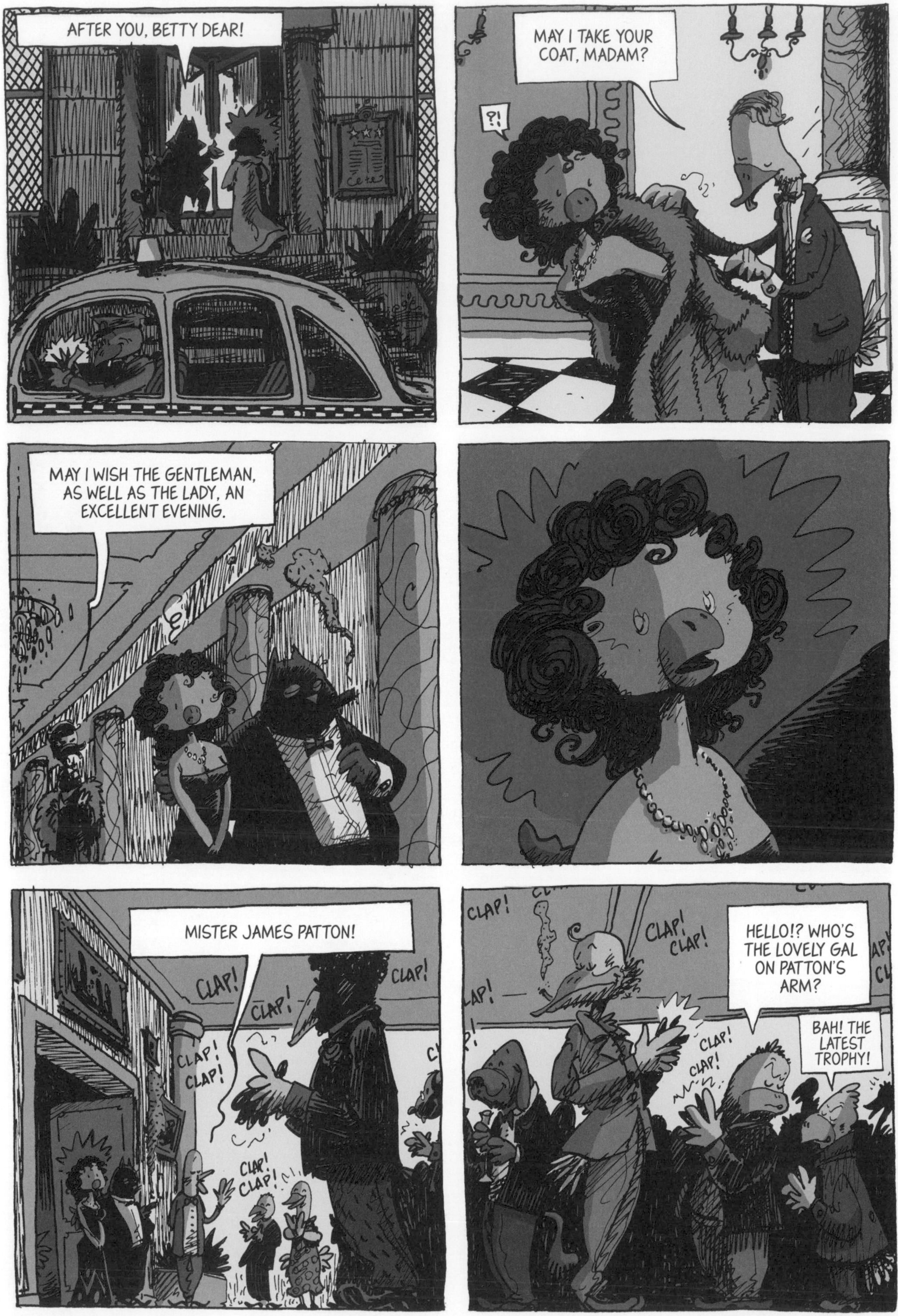
AFTER YOU, BETTY DEAR!
MAY I TAKE YOUR COAT, MADAM?
?!
MAY I WISH THE GENTLEMAN, AS WELL AS THE LADY, AN EXCELLENT EVENING.
MISTER JAMES PATTON!
CLAP!
CLAP!
CLAP!
CLAP! CLAP!
CLAP! CLAP!
CLAP!
CLAP! CLAP!
CLAP! CLAP!
HELLO!? WHO'S THE LOVELY GAL ON PATTON'S ARM?
BAH! THE LATEST TROPHY!

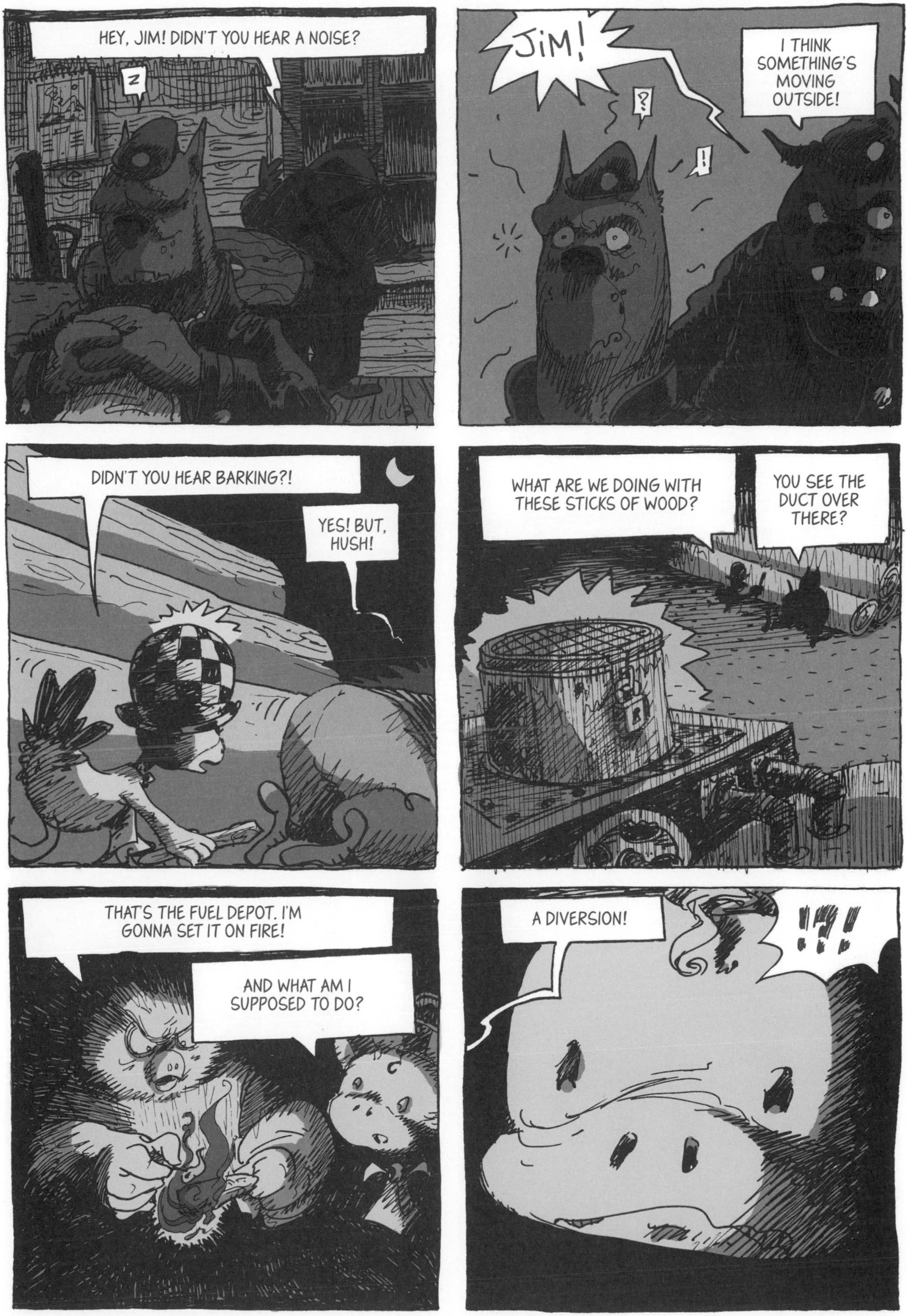
HEY, JIM! DIDN'T YOU HEAR A NOISE?
Z
JIM!
?
!
I THINK SOMETHING'S MOVING OUTSIDE!
DIDN'T YOU HEAR BARKING?!
YES! BUT, HUSH!
WHAT ARE WE DOING WITH THESE STICKS OF WOOD?
YOU SEE THE DUCT OVER THERE?
THAT'S THE FUEL DEPOT. I'M GONNA SET IT ON FIRE!
AND WHAT AM I SUPPOSED TO DO?
A DIVERSION!
!?!

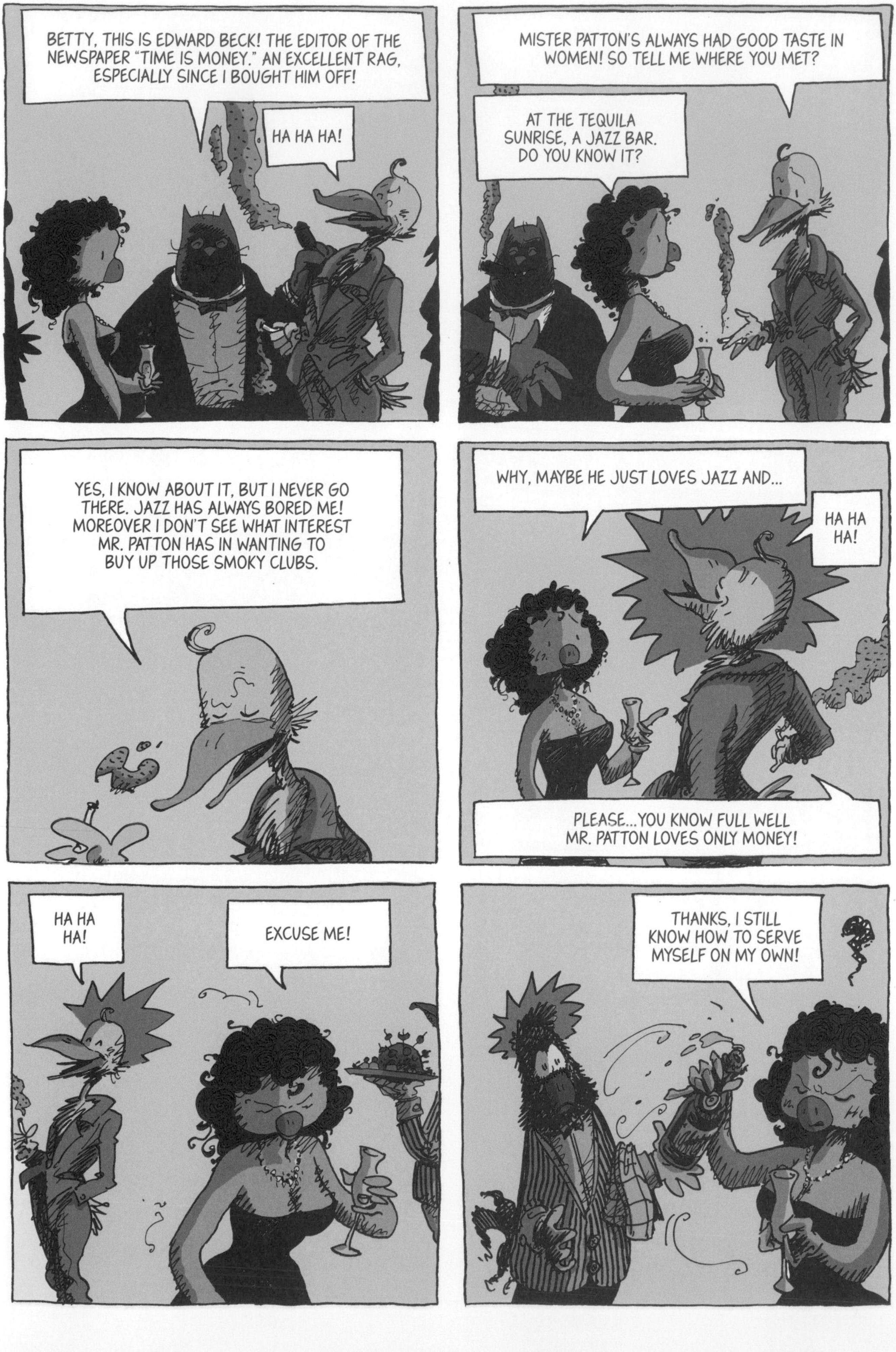
BETTY, THIS IS EDWARD BECK! THE EDITOR OF THE NEWSPAPER "TIME IS MONEY." AN EXCELLENT RAG, ESPECIALLY SINCE I BOUGHT HIM OFF!
HA HA HA!
MISTER PATTON'S ALWAYS HAD GOOD TASTE IN WOMEN! SO TELL ME WHERE YOU MET?
AT THE TEQUILA SUNRISE, A JAZZ BAR. DO YOU KNOW IT?
YES, I KNOW ABOUT IT, BUT I NEVER GO THERE. JAZZ HAS ALWAYS BORED ME! MOREOVER I DON'T SEE WHAT INTEREST MR. PATTON HAS IN WANTING TO BUY UP THOSE SMOKY CLUBS.
WHY, MAYBE HE JUST LOVES JAZZ AND...
HA HA HA!
PLEASE...YOU KNOW FULL WELL MR. PATTON LOVES ONLY MONEY!
HA HA HA!
EXCUSE ME!
THANKS, I STILL KNOW HOW TO SERVE MYSELF ON MY OWN!

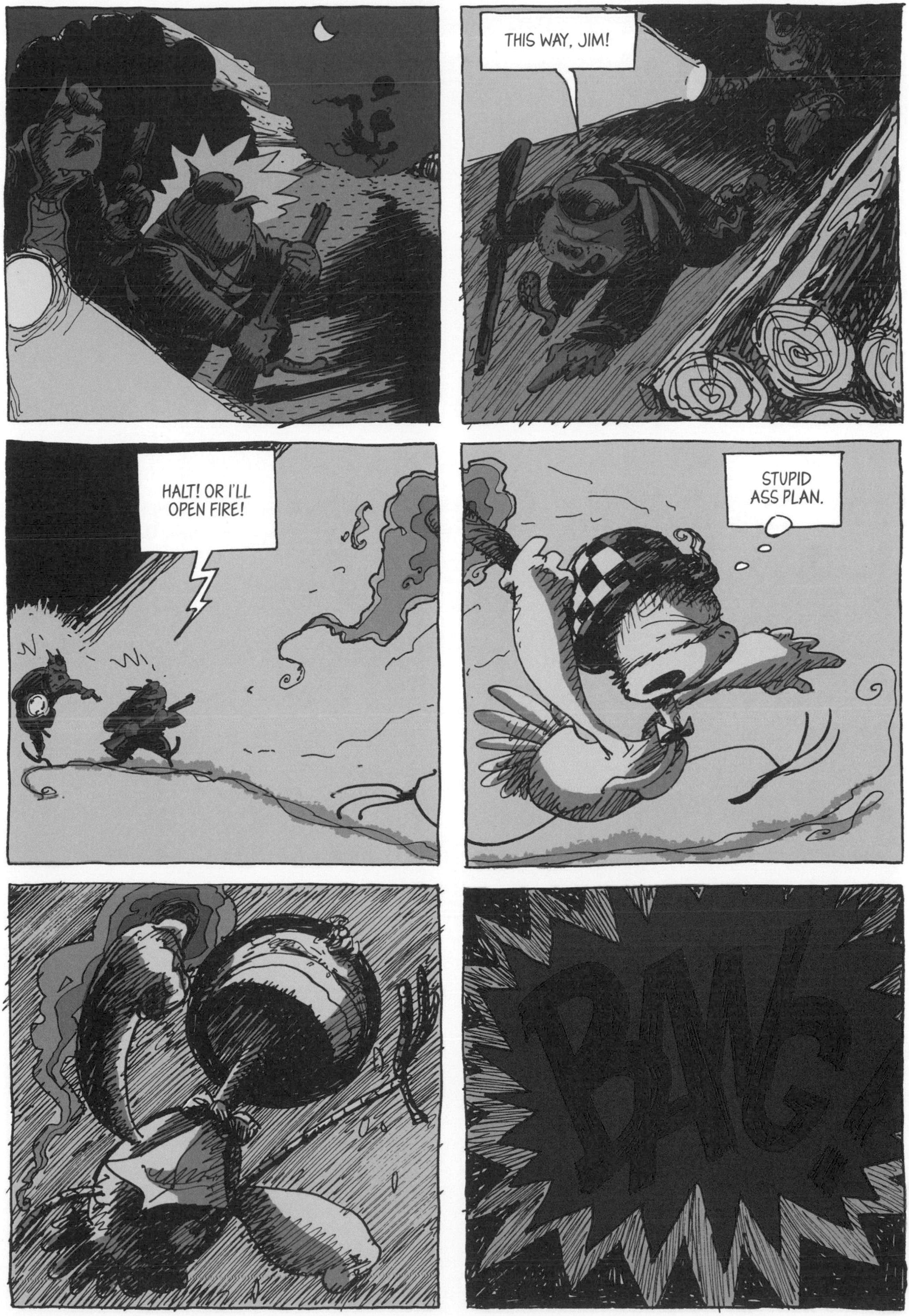
THIS WAY, JIM!
HALT! OR I'LL OPEN FIRE!
STUPID ASS PLAN.
BANG!

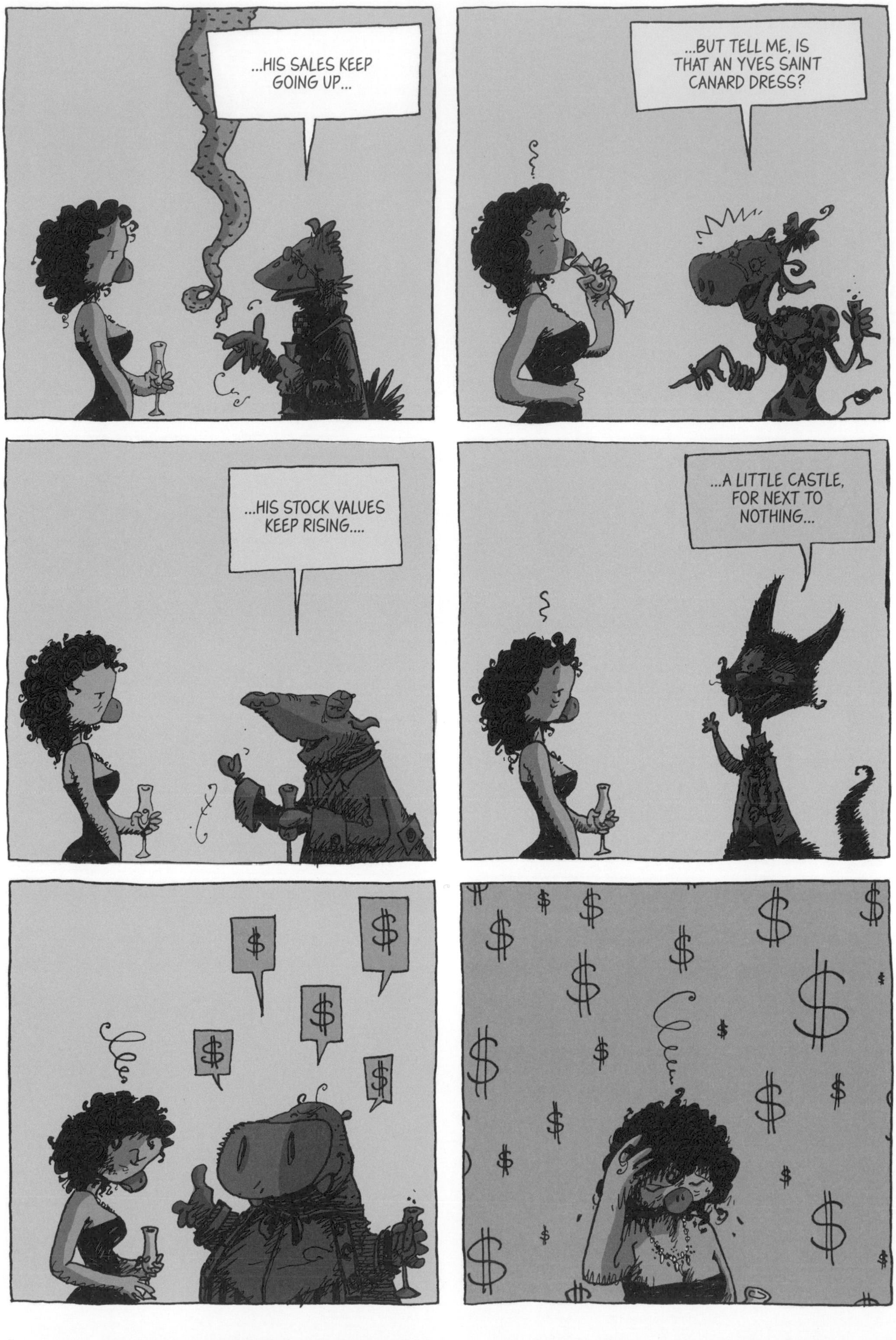
...HIS SALES KEEP GOING UP...
...BUT TELL ME, IS THAT AN YVES SAINT CANARD DRESS?
...HIS STOCK VALUES KEEP RISING....
...A LITTLE CASTLE, FOR NEXT TO NOTHING...

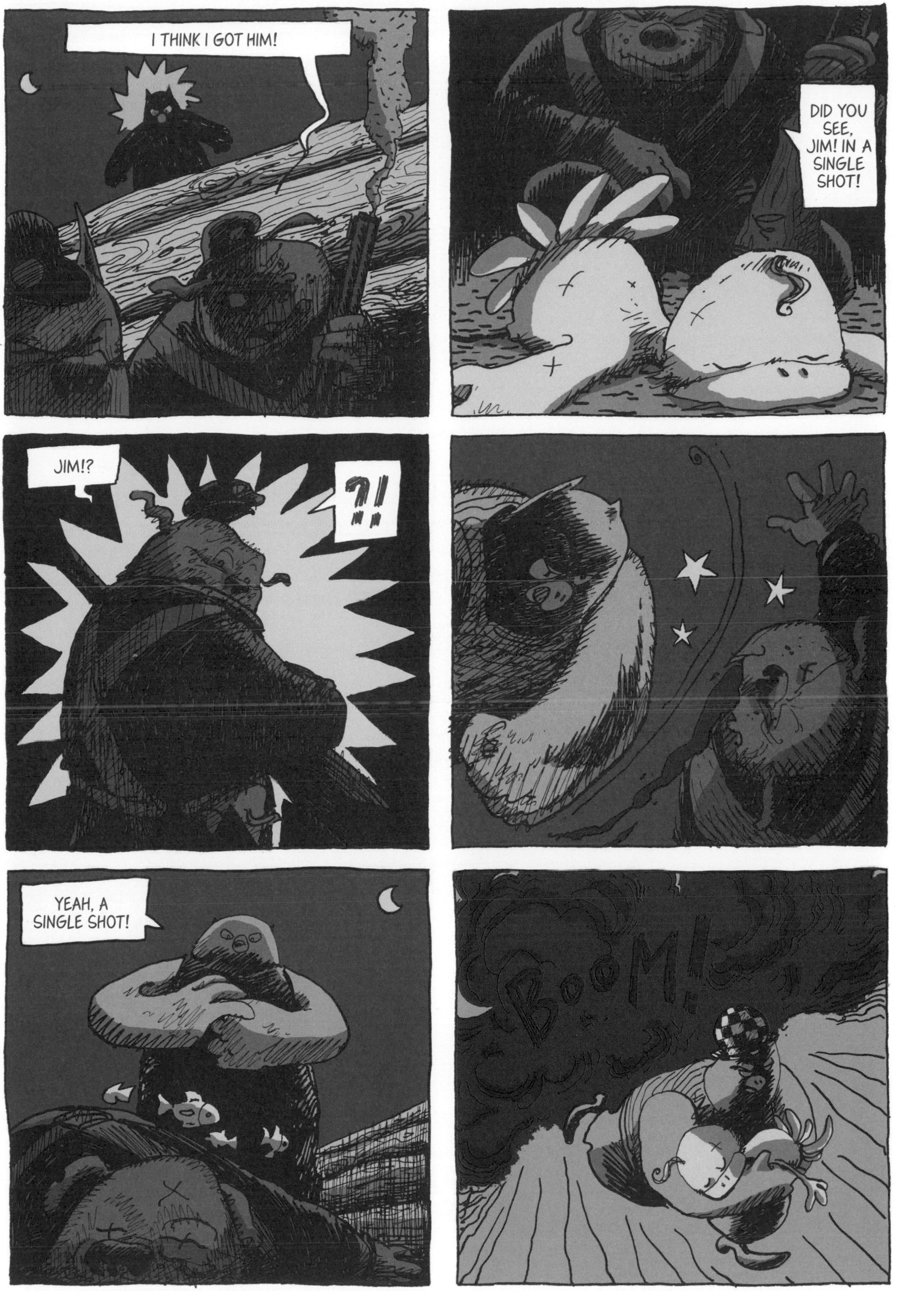

I THINK I GOT HIM!
DID YOU SEE, JIM! IN A SINGLE SHOT!
JIM!?
?!
YEAH, A SINGLE SHOT!
BOOM!

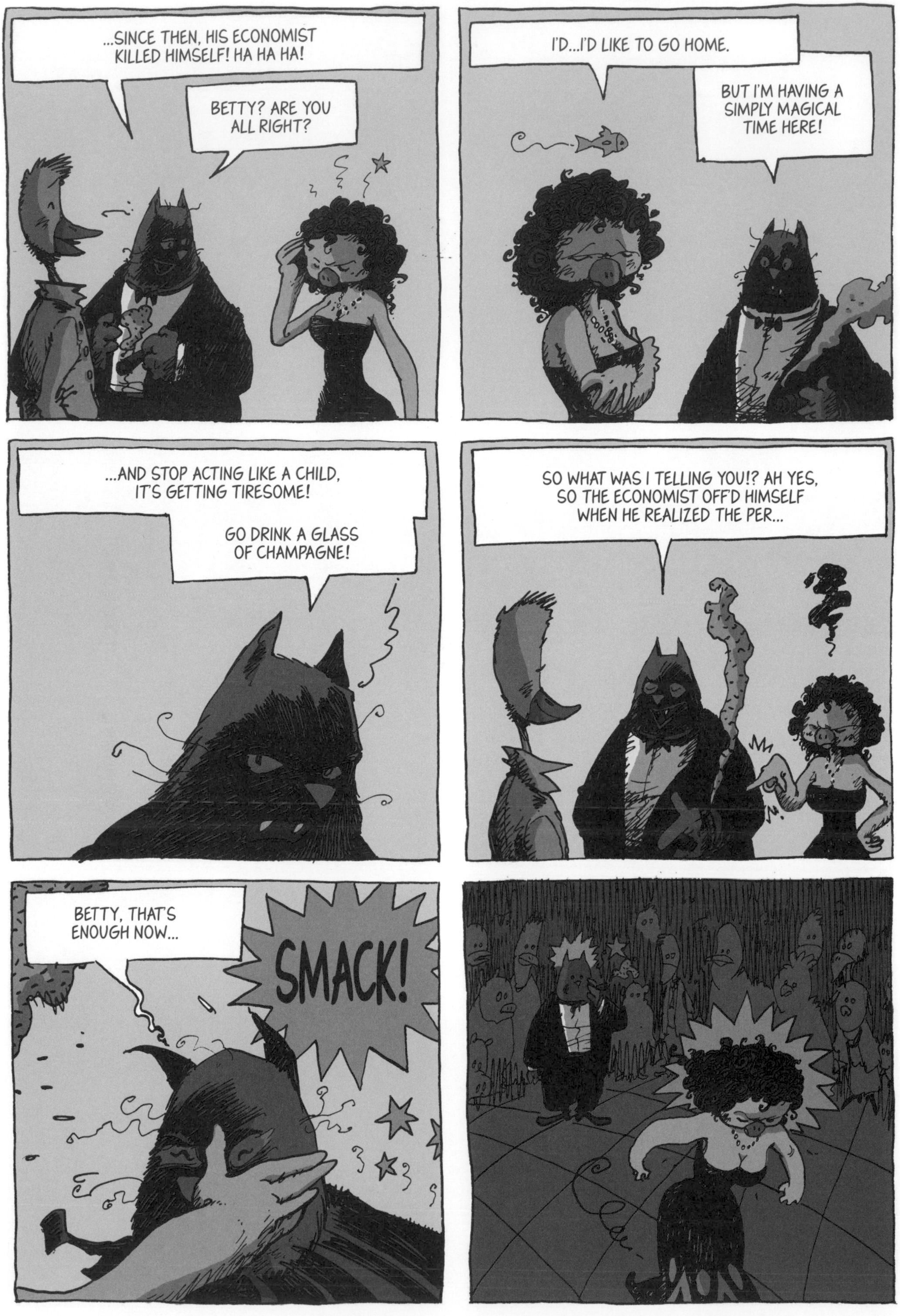
...SINCE THEN, HIS ECONOMIST KILLED HIMSELF! HA HA HA!
BETTY? ARE YOU ALL RIGHT?
I'D...I'D LIKE TO GO HOME.
BUT I'M HAVING A SIMPLY MAGICAL TIME HERE!
...AND STOP ACTING LIKE A CHILD, IT'S GETTING TIRESOME!
GO DRINK A GLASS OF CHAMPAGNE!
SO WHAT WAS I TELLING YOU!? AH YES, SO THE ECONOMIST OFF'D HIMSELF WHEN HE REALIZED THE PER...
BETTY, THAT'S ENOUGH NOW...
SMACK!

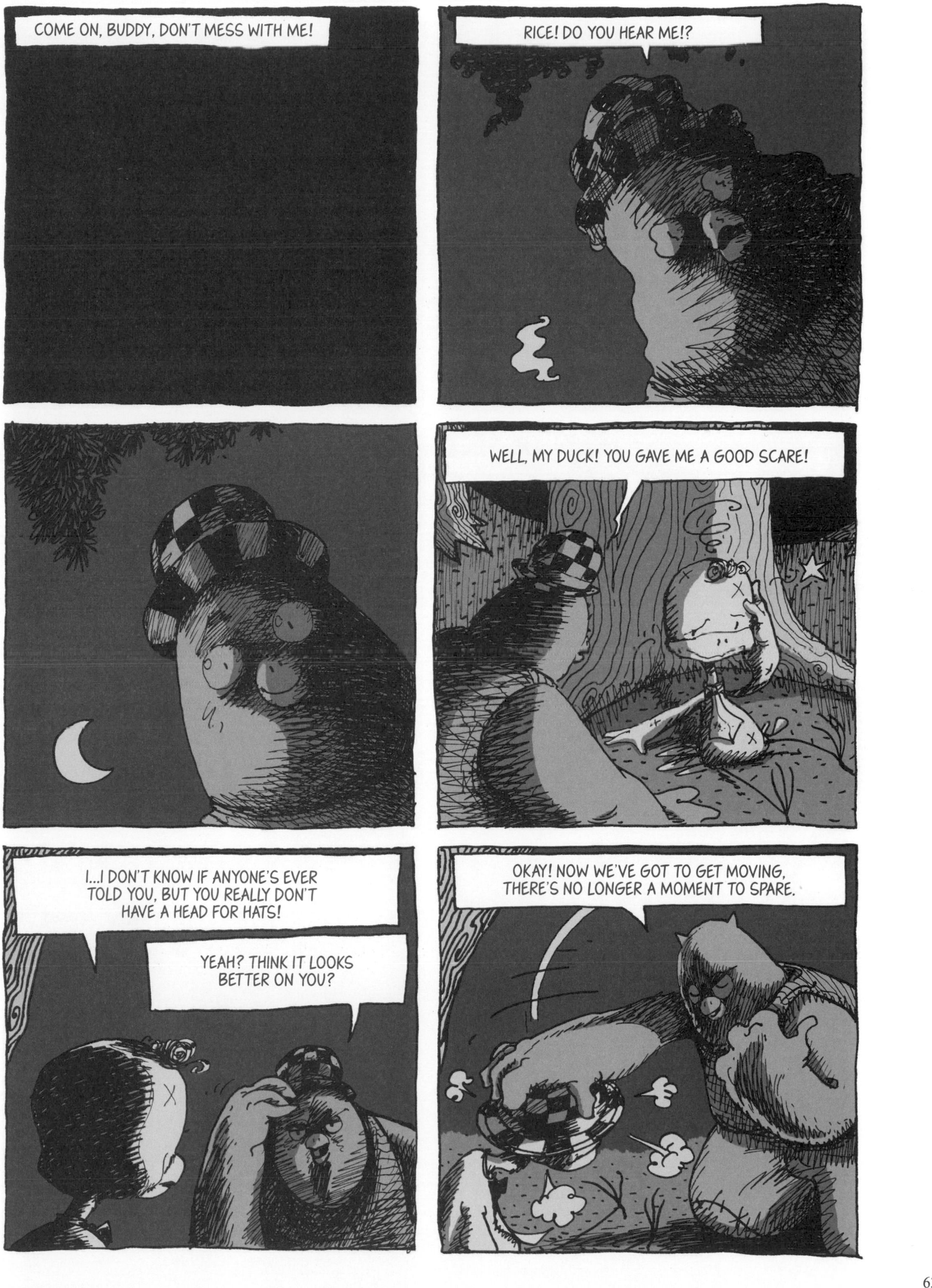
COME ON, BUDDY, DON'T MESS WITH ME!
RICE! DO YOU HEAR ME!?
WELL, MY DUCK! YOU GAVE ME A GOOD SCARE!
I...I DON'T KNOW IF ANYONE'S EVER TOLD YOU, BUT YOU REALLY DON'T HAVE A HEAD FOR HATS!
YEAH? THINK IT LOOKS BETTER ON YOU?
OKAY! NOW WE'VE GOT TO GET MOVING, THERE'S NO LONGER A MOMENT TO SPARE.

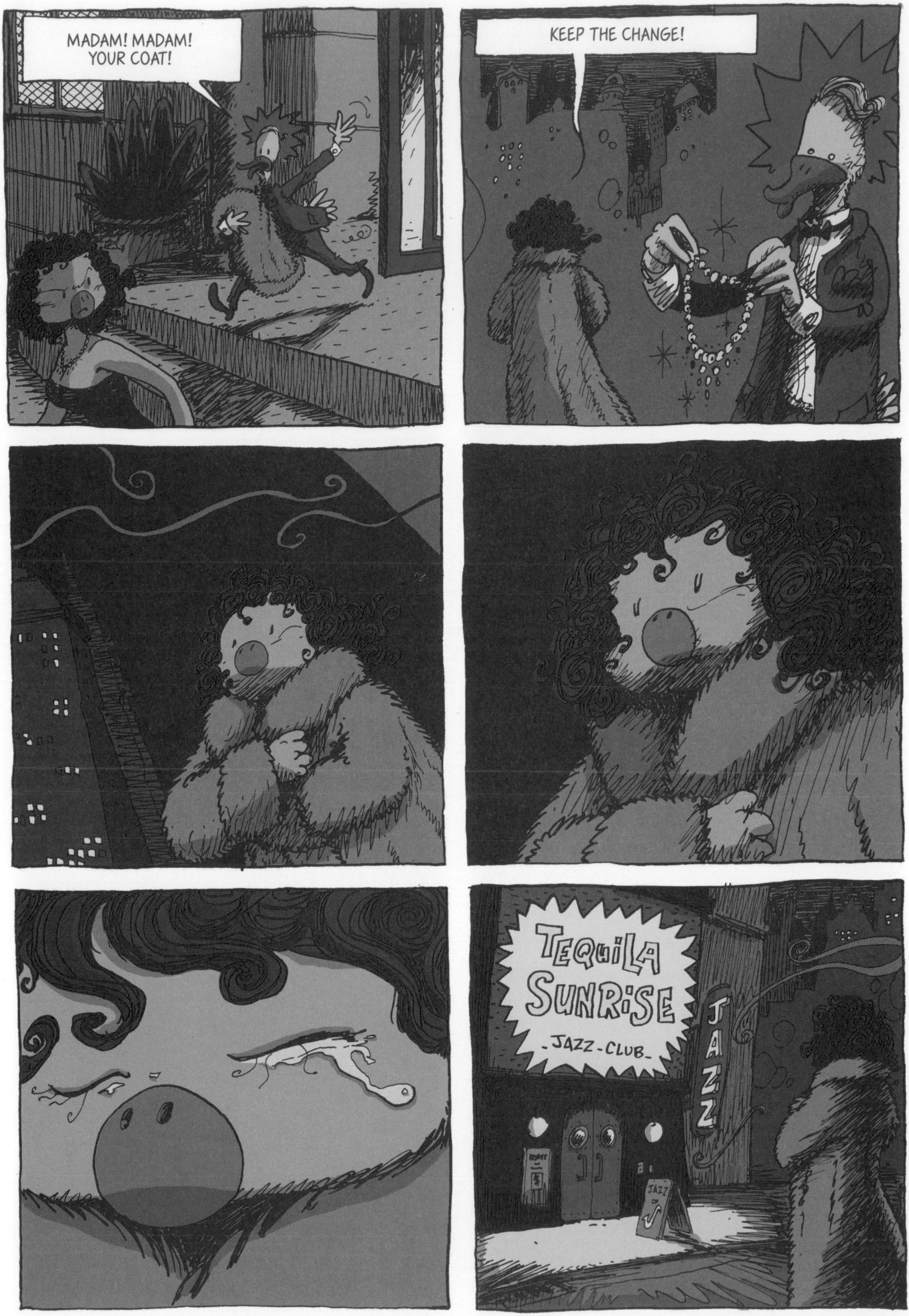
MADAM! MADAM! YOUR COAT!
KEEP THE CHANGE!
TEQUILA SUNRISE
-JAZZ-CLUB-
JAZZ
JAZZ

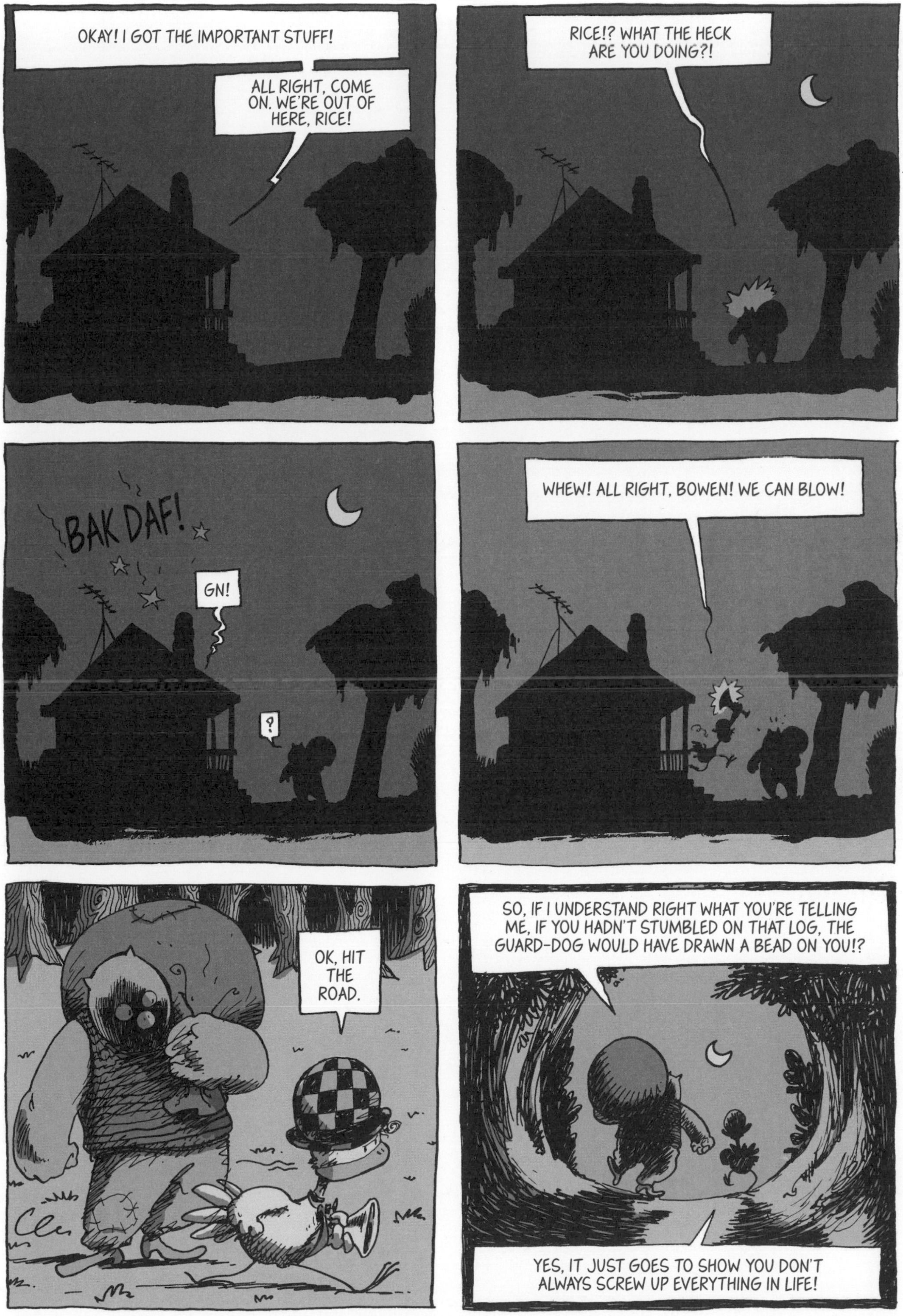

OKAY! I GOT THE IMPORTANT STUFF!
ALL RIGHT, COME ON. WE'RE OUT OF HERE, RICE!
RICE!? WHAT THE HECK ARE YOU DOING?!
BAK DAF!
GN!
?
WHEW! ALL RIGHT, BOWEN! WE CAN BLOW!
OK, HIT THE ROAD.
SO, IF I UNDERSTAND RIGHT WHAT YOU'RE TELLING ME, IF YOU HADN'T STUMBLED ON THAT LOG, THE GUARD-DOG WOULD HAVE DRAWN A BEAD ON YOU!?
YES, IT JUST GOES TO SHOW YOU DON'T ALWAYS SCREW UP EVERYTHING IN LIFE!

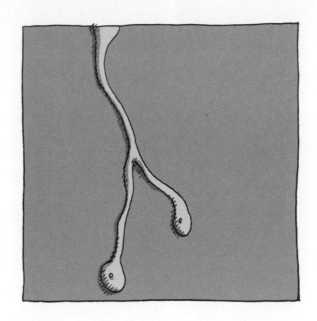

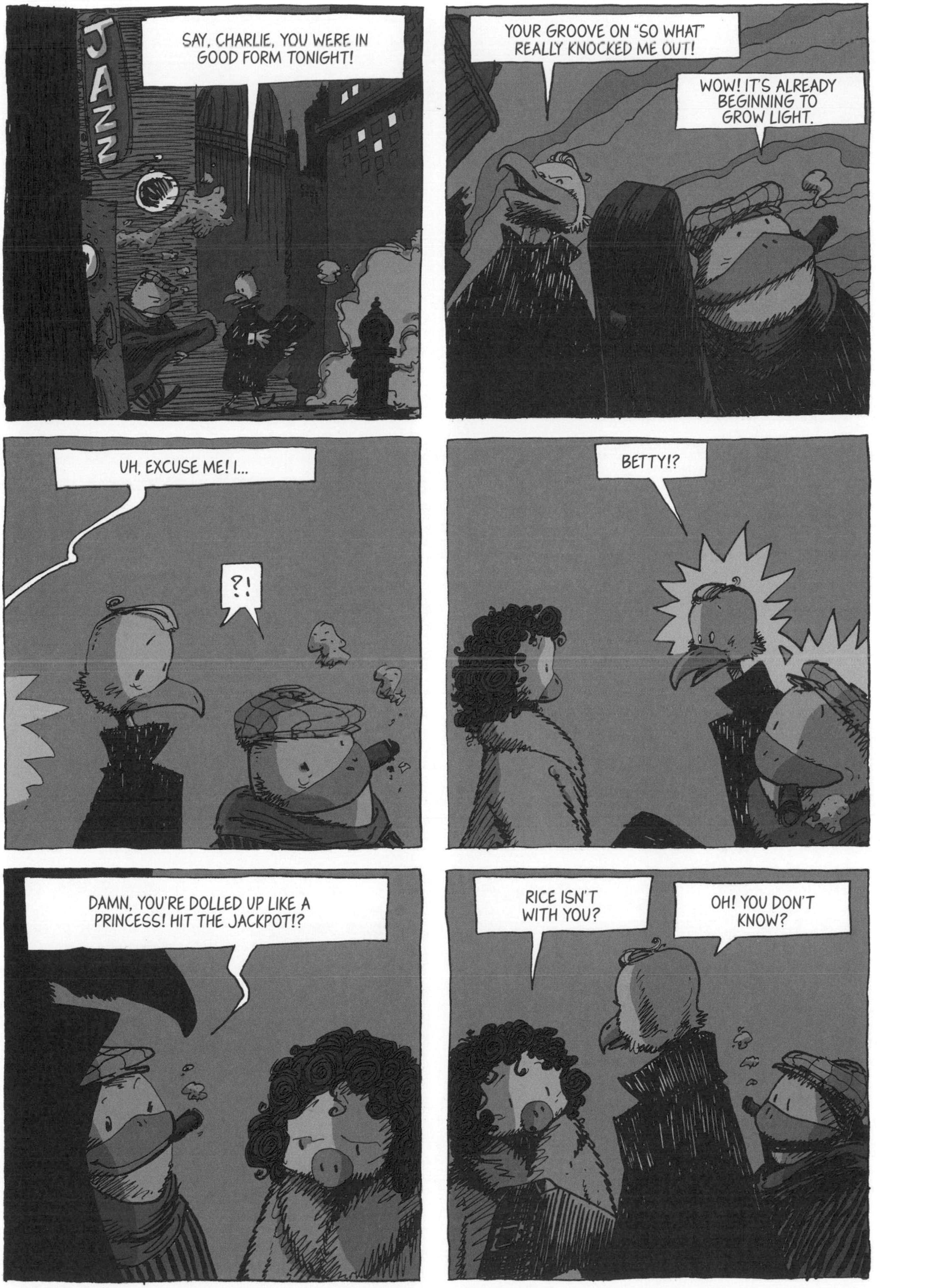

JAZZ
SAY, CHARLIE, YOU WERE IN GOOD FORM TONIGHT!
YOUR GROOVE ON "SO WHAT" REALLY KNOCKED ME OUT!
WOW! IT'S ALREADY BEGINNING TO GROW LIGHT.
UH, EXCUSE ME! I...
?!
BETTY!?
DAMN, YOU'RE DOLLED UP LIKE A PRINCESS! HIT THE JACKPOT!?
RICE ISN'T WITH YOU?
OH! YOU DON'T KNOW?

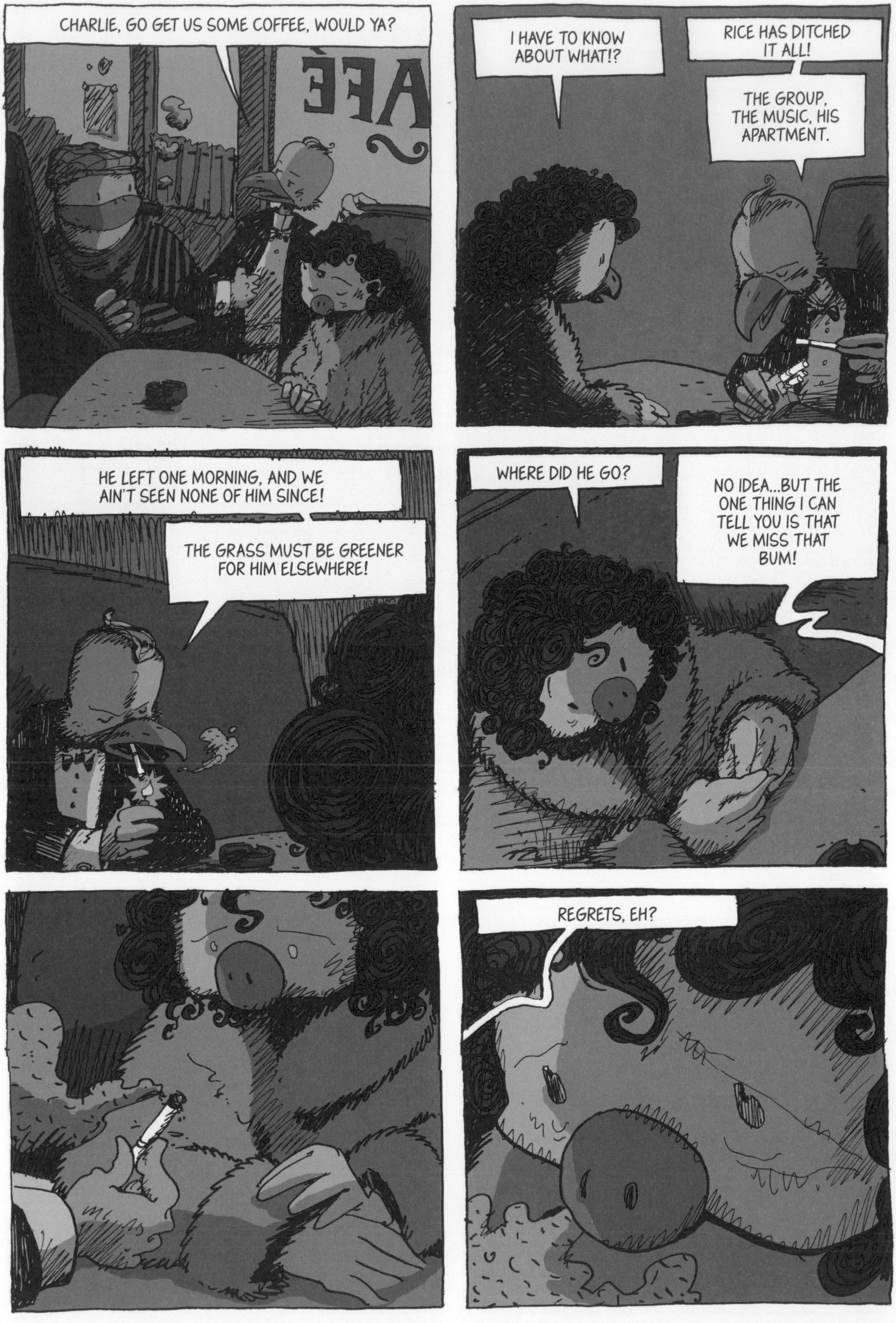
CHARLIE, GO GET US SOME COFFEE, WOULD YA?
AFÉ
I HAVE TO KNOW ABOUT WHAT!?
RICE HAS DITCHED IT ALL!
THE GROUP, THE MUSIC, HIS APARTMENT.
HE LEFT ONE MORNING, AND WE AIN'T SEEN NONE OF HIM SINCE!
THE GRASS MUST BE GREENER FOR HIM ELSEWHERE!
WHERE DID HE GO?
NO IDEA...BUT THE ONE THING I CAN TELL YOU IS THAT WE MISS THAT BUM!
REGRETS, EH?

BELIEVE ME! EVEN IF I HAVE TO GO TO EVERY JAZZ BAR IN THE COUNTRY, I'LL FIND HIM AGAIN!

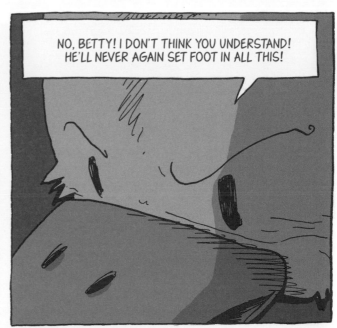

NO, BETTY! I DON'T THINK YOU UNDERSTAND! HE'LL NEVER AGAIN SET FOOT IN ALL THIS!

I DON'T BELIEVE YOU! NOT RICE...NOT HIM!

LISTEN, HE EVEN THREW HIS TRUMPET INTO THE WATER.

I'LL...I'LL FIND HIM AGAIN!

DID YOU SAY SOMETHING STUPID?!

NO! SHE'S THE ONE WHO REALLY SCREWED UP!

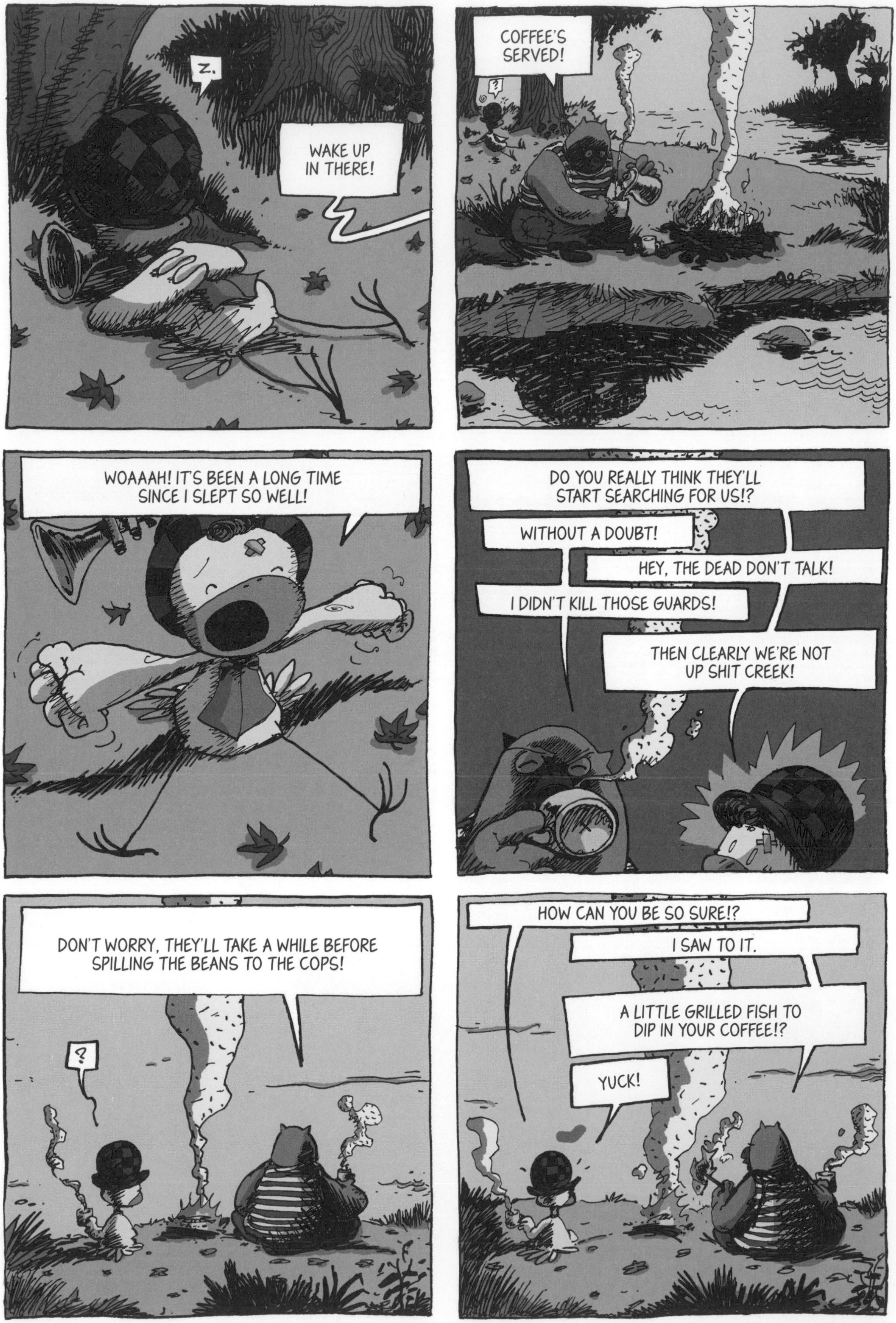
Z.
WAKE UP IN THERE!
COFFEE'S SERVED!
?
WOAAAH! IT'S BEEN A LONG TIME SINCE I SLEPT SO WELL!
DO YOU REALLY THINK THEY'LL START SEARCHING FOR US!?
WITHOUT A DOUBT!
HEY, THE DEAD DON'T TALK!
I DIDN'T KILL THOSE GUARDS!
THEN CLEARLY WE'RE NOT UP SHIT CREEK!
DON'T WORRY, THEY'LL TAKE A WHILE BEFORE SPILLING THE BEANS TO THE COPS!
?
HOW CAN YOU BE SO SURE!?
I SAW TO IT.
A LITTLE GRILLED FISH TO DIP IN YOUR COFFEE!?
YUCK!

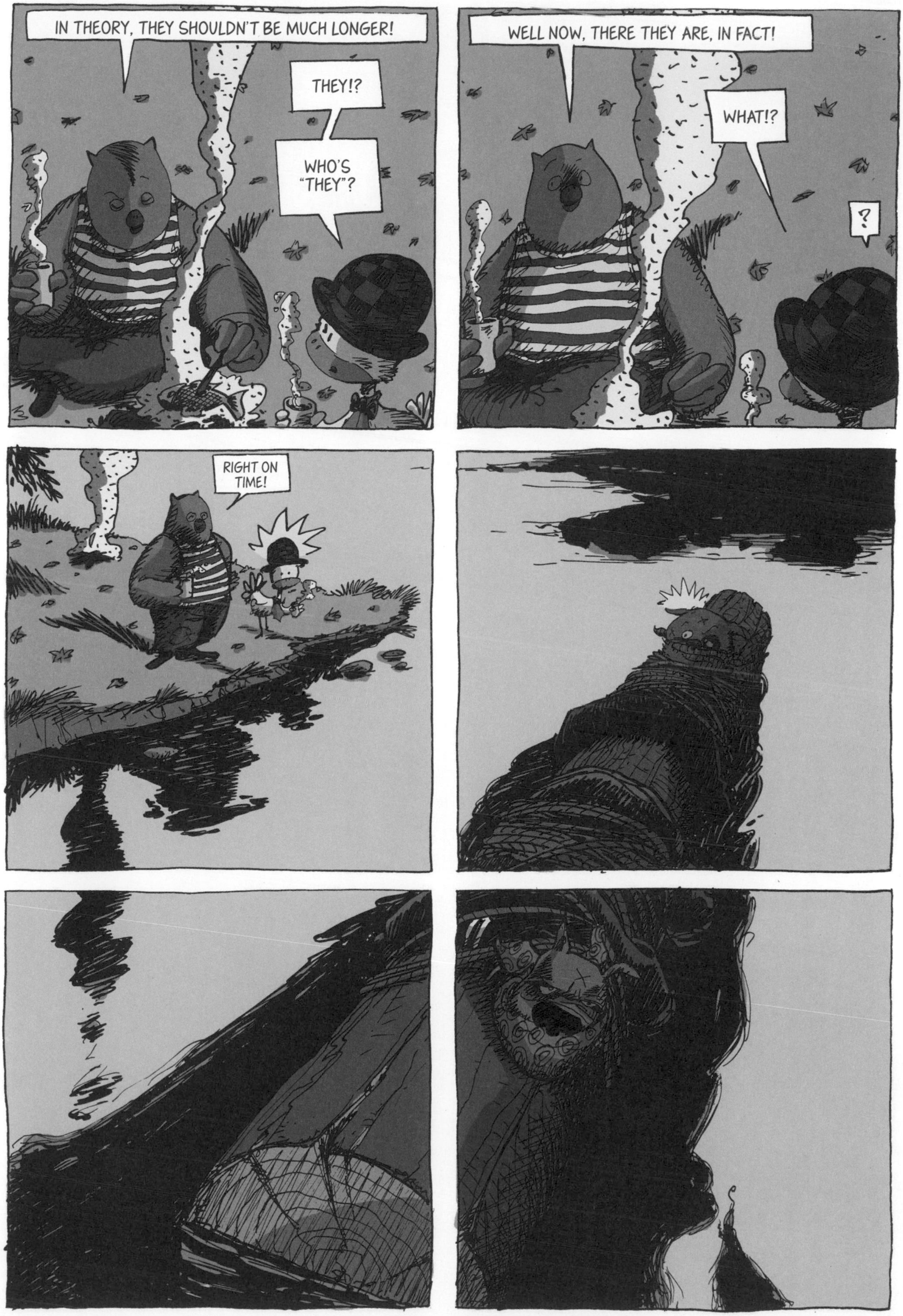
IN THEORY, THEY SHOULDN'T BE MUCH LONGER!
THEY!?
WHO'S "THEY"?
WELL NOW, THERE THEY ARE, IN FACT!
WHAT!?
?
RIGHT ON TIME!

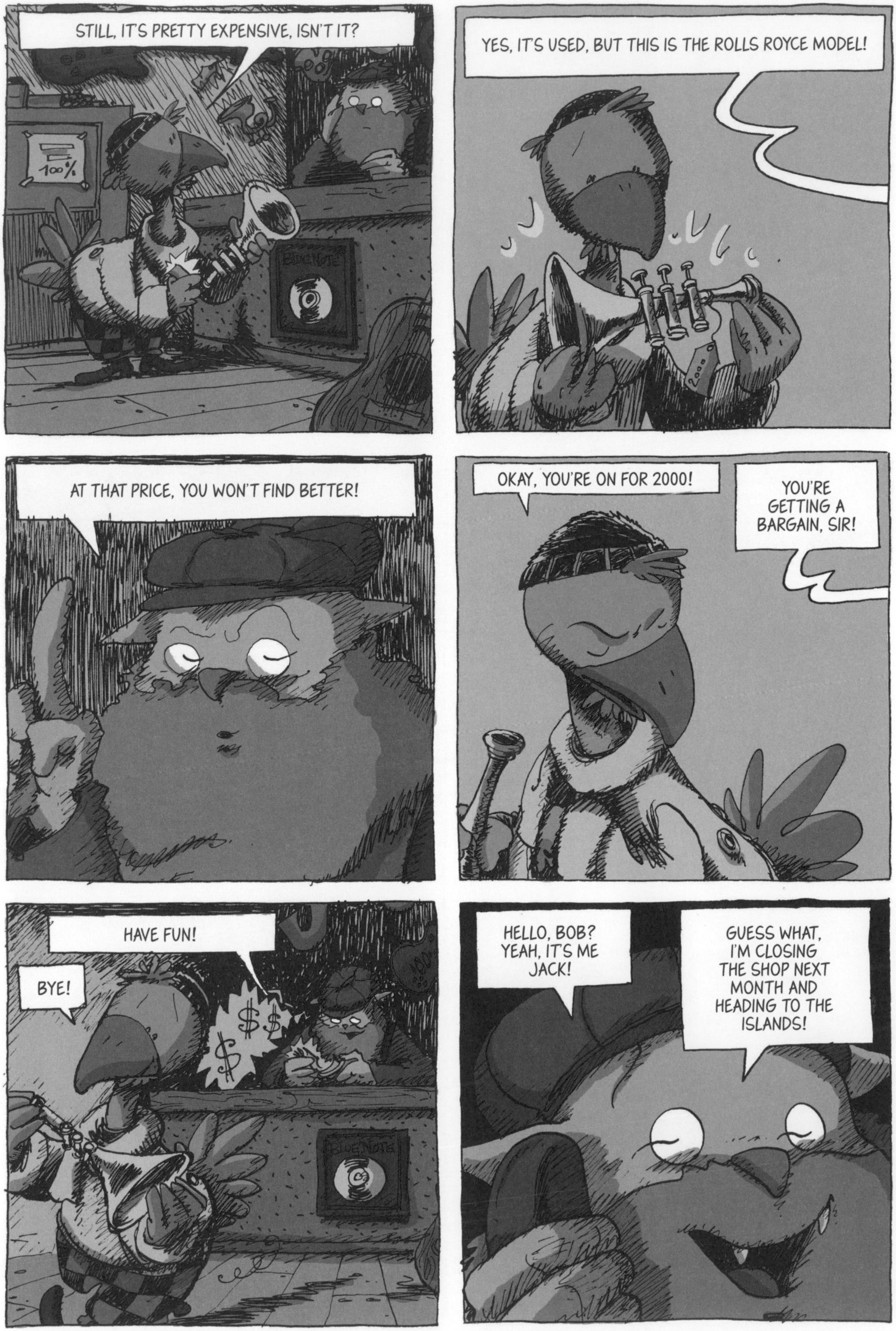
STILL, IT'S PRETTY EXPENSIVE, ISN'T IT?
YES, IT'S USED, BUT THIS IS THE ROLLS ROYCE MODEL!
AT THAT PRICE, YOU WON'T FIND BETTER!
OKAY, YOU'RE ON FOR 2000!
YOU'RE GETTING A BARGAIN, SIR!
HAVE FUN!
BYE!
HELLO, BOB? YEAH, IT'S ME JACK!
GUESS WHAT, I'M CLOSING THE SHOP NEXT MONTH AND HEADING TO THE ISLANDS!

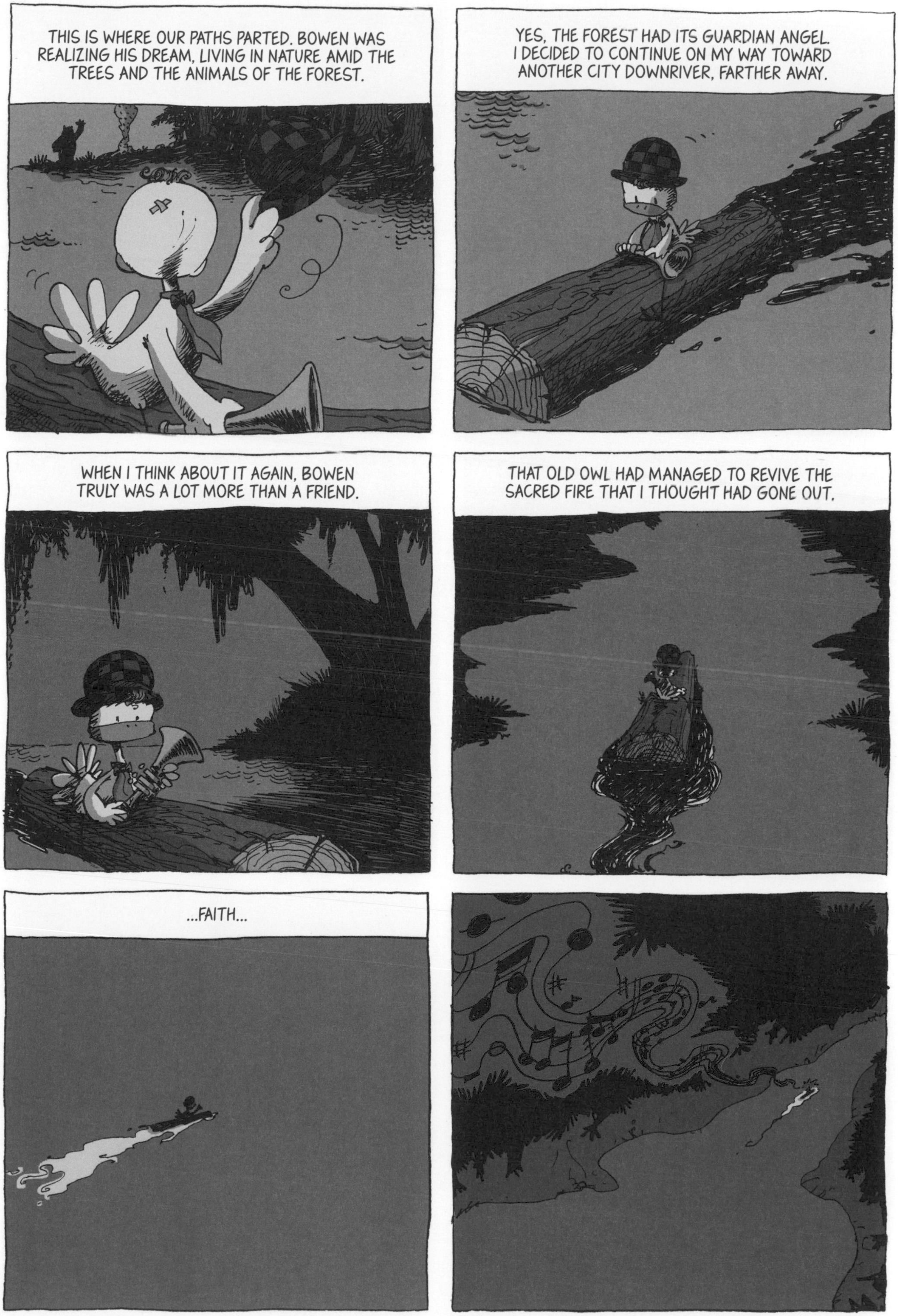
THIS IS WHERE OUR PATHS PARTED. BOWEN WAS REALIZING HIS DREAM, LIVING IN NATURE AMID THE TREES AND THE ANIMALS OF THE FOREST.
YES, THE FOREST HAD ITS GUARDIAN ANGEL. I DECIDED TO CONTINUE ON MY WAY TOWARD ANOTHER CITY DOWNRIVER, FARTHER AWAY.
WHEN I THINK ABOUT IT AGAIN, BOWEN TRULY WAS A LOT MORE THAN A FRIEND.
THAT OLD OWL HAD MANAGED TO REVIVE THE SACRED FIRE THAT I THOUGHT HAD GONE OUT.
...FAITH...

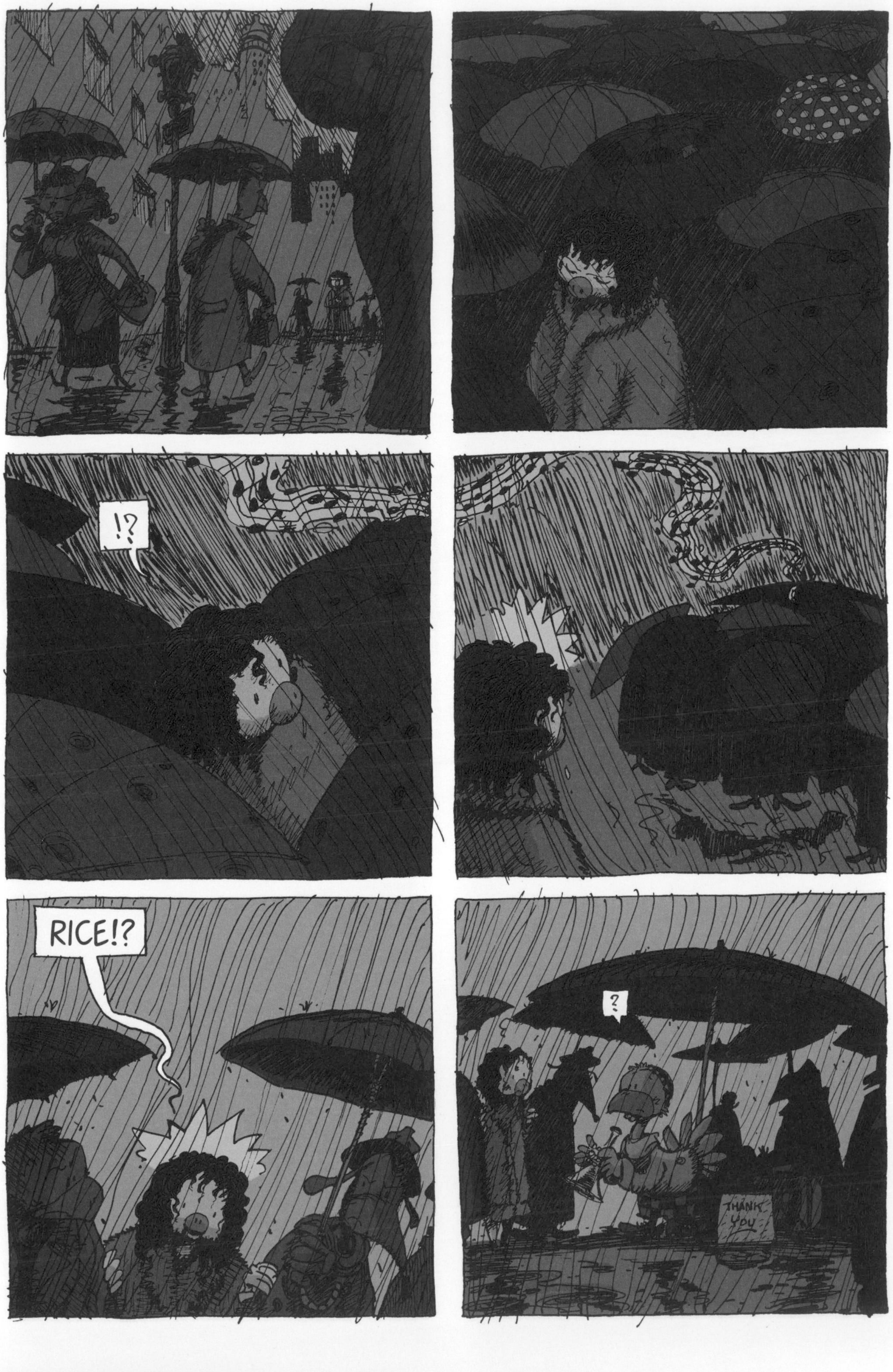
!?
RICE!?
?
THANK YOU

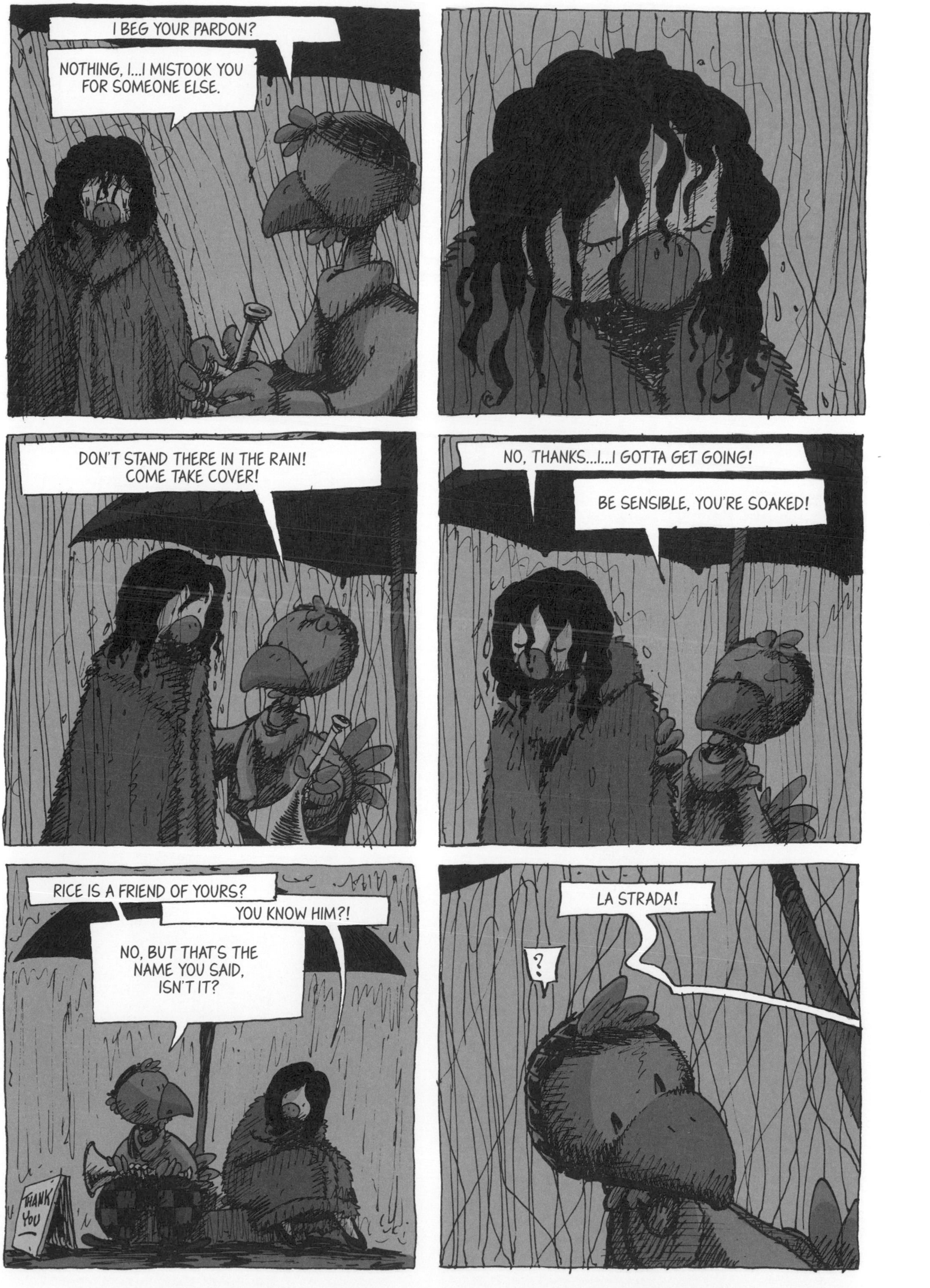
I BEG YOUR PARDON?
NOTHING, I...I MISTOOK YOU FOR SOMEONE ELSE.
DON'T STAND THERE IN THE RAIN! COME TAKE COVER!
NO, THANKS...I...I GOTTA GET GOING!
BE SENSIBLE, YOU'RE SOAKED!
RICE IS A FRIEND OF YOURS?
YOU KNOW HIM?!
NO, BUT THAT'S THE NAME YOU SAID, ISN'T IT?
THANK YOU
LA STRADA!
?

YES, THE MUSIC FOR THE MOVIE "LA STRADA." THAT WAS THE TUNE YOU WERE PLAYING, WASN'T IT?

UH, YEAH, RIGHT.

RICE WOULD OFTEN PLAY THAT TUNE TO MAKE ME HAPPY!

...

ISN'T IT THE STORY OF A GUY WHO, TO MAKE HIS LIVING, BREAKS OUT OF CHAINS...SOMETHING LIKE THAT?

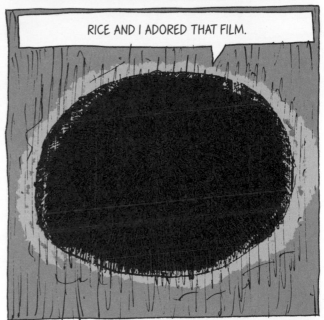

RICE AND I ADORED THAT FILM.

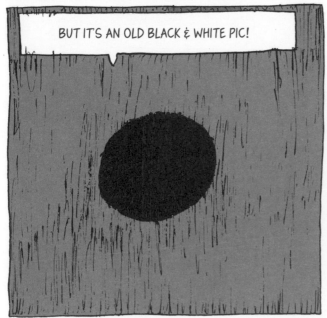

BUT IT'S AN OLD BLACK & WHITE PIC!

YES, BUT INSIDE IT THERE ARE THE COLORS OF A CHAGALL!

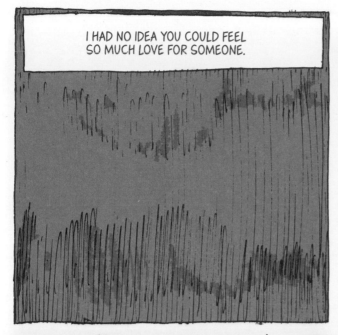

I HAD NO IDEA YOU COULD FEEL SO MUCH LOVE FOR SOMEONE.

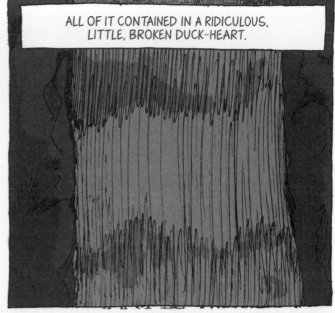

ALL OF IT CONTAINED IN A RIDICULOUS, LITTLE, BROKEN DUCK-HEART.

THAT'S WHY, DESPITE HEARTBREAK, LIFE REMAINS SO BEAUTIFUL.

WE'RE SO INSIGNIFICANT IN THIS WORLD AND YET WE'RE CAPABLE OF EXPERIENCING THINGS BRUSHING THE ETERNAL.

IN THE DEEPEST PART OF MYSELF, I KNOW THAT, ONE DAY, BETTY AND I WILL FIND EACH OTHER AGAIN...BUT, CERTAINLY, IN ANOTHER LIFE.

EVEN IF I'M CONVINCED REINCARNATION IS HOGWASH.

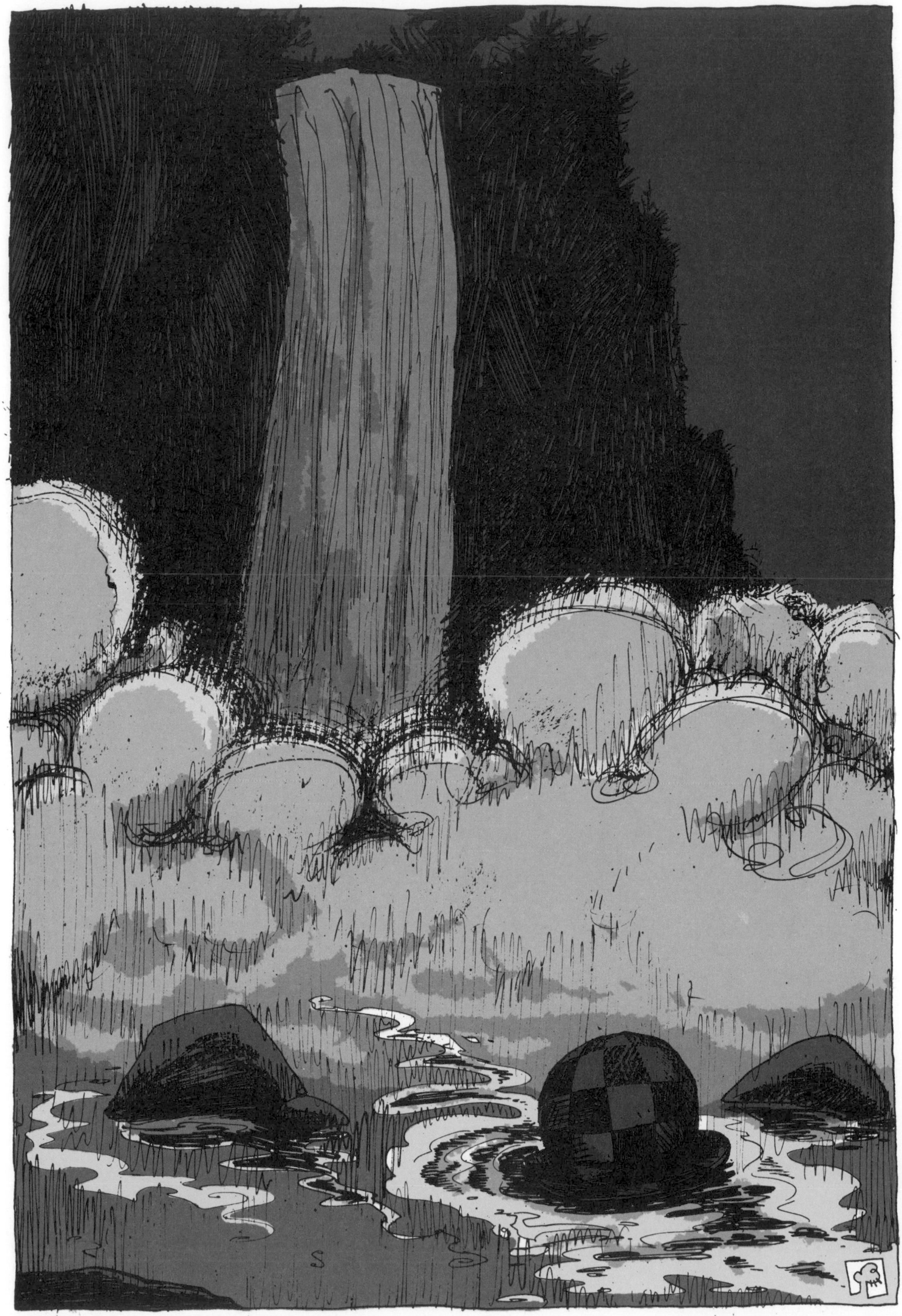